Creative Interventions
for
Children of Divorce

Liana Lowenstein

Champion Press
Toronto

Library and Archives Canada Cataloguing in Publication

Lowenstein, Liana, 1965-
        Creative interventions for children of divorce / Liana Lowenstein.

Includes bibliographical references.
ISBN 0-9685199-3-8

1.   Children of divorced parents-counseling of. 2. Child psychotherapy. 3. Group counseling for children. I. Title.

HQ777.5.L682006   618.92'8914   C2006-902982-2

Correspondence regarding this book can be sent to:
Liana Lowenstein c/o Champion Press
Pharma Plus, PO Box 91012, 2901 Bayview Avenue, Toronto, Ontario, Canada M2K 2Y6
Telephone: 416-575-7836 Fax: 416-756-7201
Email: liana@globalserve.net Web: lianalowenstein.com

Acknowledgments

My heartfelt thanks are due first to the children and parents I have worked with over the years, for the many lessons they have taught me. They are the true inspiration for this book.

I owe a tremendous debt of gratitude to Marlin Kriss, Teri Krull, Helen Radovanovic, and Anita Trubitt, who so generously donated their time to review my manuscript, providing me with valuable suggestions and encouragement. I am grateful to the colleagues who graciously took the time to try the activities with their clients, and who offered helpful feedback. I thank Vicki Lansky for her words of support. I also thank Lorraine Martin from the Office of the Children's Lawyer, for her guidance over the years.

Thanks to Fern Rubinstein and Robyn Naster, for their editorial assistance, and Lisa Stein, for proofreading the manuscript. Thanks also to the staff at Hignell Book Printing, for their help in preparing this manuscript.

Special gratitude is expressed to my family and friends for their continued support and encouragement. I am particularly thankful to my husband, Steven, for his love and understanding, and to my daughter Jaime, for the joy she brings to my life.

Liana Lowenstein
June 2006

Introduction

Many children are referred for therapy to help them adjust to divorce. They typically feel vulnerable and overwhelmed by conflicting emotions. They may feel anxious about the therapeutic process and be reluctant to talk directly about the divorce. Activities that are creative and play-based can engage children and help them to safely express their thoughts and feelings. The purpose of this book is to provide mental health professionals who work with children of divorce with creative interventions to engage, assess, and treat them. A range of innovative activities are presented, including therapeutic games, art, puppets, role-plays, and stories. Studies have demonstrated the effectiveness of these play-based interventions for children (Utay & Lampe, 1995; Burroughs, Wagner, & Johnson, 1997; McCarthy, 1998; Johnson et al., 1998). Most of the activities in this book have been developed for children ages 7 through 12, but many can be modified for both younger and older children.

Practitioners working with children of divorce should have clinical training and a sound knowledge base in: child development, attachment theory, psychopathology, the impact of divorce on children, and play therapy for children of divorce. A list of suggested readings and professional training associations is provided at the end of the book for those who wish to broaden their knowledge. The activities presented here can be integrated into any theoretical orientation that uses a directive child therapy approach. Thus, practitioners from a wide range of theoretical orientations will find many activities to incorporate into their therapy sessions.

The first section of this book, which contains guidelines for practitioners, lays the foundation for effective counseling with children of divorce. Section Two presents a theoretical overview on children of divorce and incorporates some of the latest literature on the topic. Additional reading can be found in the *References and Suggested Reading* section. The third section provides material for use with the child's parents. It includes a letter to give parents in the first session, informing them about the therapeutic process, and a social history questionnaire to be used as part of the clinical assessment. A handout, *Helping Your Children through Separation and Divorce,* is also included, which will help parents better understand and respond to their child. The remaining sections offer assessment and treatment tools and interventions. In addition to individual therapy activities, there are also interventions for children's divorce groups and family sessions. An overview for practitioners is presented at the beginning of each section to provide clinical guidelines for how to use the interventions. The Appendix includes a Custody/Access Dispute Contract; a treatment plan; a sample letter for the practitioner to give to the child upon termination from therapy; and resources for children, parents, and professionals.

The interventions in this book have been specially designed to capture and sustain children's interest and motivation in therapy, and to help children deal with the divorce within the context of a safe and neutral therapeutic environment. Practitioners can make an enormous difference in the lives of children of divorce by providing them with a positive and engaging therapeutic experience.

Contents

Section 6 – Interventions to Process Emotional and Behavioral Reactions 101

Section 7 – Interventions to Facilitate Coping and Enhance Self-Esteem 127

Section 8 – Interventions for Group Sessions 143

Section 9 – Interventions for Family Sessions 159

Activities at a Glance

ACTIVITY	GOAL	AGES	MODALITY
Feel Better Bag	Implement adaptive coping techniques	7-12	I,G
About Me	Begin to articulate thoughts and feelings	7-12	I,G
Getting To Know Each Other	Establish therapeutic rapport	7-12	I
Feeling Faces Cut 'N Paste	Identify range of feelings regarding the divorce	7-10	I,G
Feelings Tic-Tac-Toe	Identify a range of different feelings	7-12	I,F
My Parents' Divorce Dice Game	Verbalize feelings and reactions regarding divorce	7-12	I,G
How I Think, Feel, and Behave	Identify stresses, symptoms, coping strategies	7-12	I
Butterflies in My Stomach	Identify stresses, supports, problem-solving	7-12	I
People in My World	Identify feelings toward self, family, community	7-12	I
Life's Ups & Downs	Identify positive and negative life events	8-16	I
Time with my Mother and Father	Express thoughts and feelings regarding parents	7-12	I
Marriage and Divorce	Verbalize an understanding of divorce	6-12	I,G
Divorce: How It Works	Verbalize an understanding of divorce	8-12	I,G
My Parents Love Me Forever	Verbalize feeling loved by both parents	7-10	I,F
Changes in My Life	Identify positive and negative changes since divorce	8-12	I
Going Back & Forth Air Hockey	Implement adaptive coping techniques	7-12	I
Luggage Tag	Implement adaptive coping techniques	7-12	I,G,F
My Parents Argue	Identify ways to deal with parental conflict	7-12	I
Caught in the Middle Scribble Game	Verbalize feelings of being caught in the middle	7-12	I
My Parents are Fighting Over Me	Identify ways to deal with parental conflict	7-10	I
Wish Parents Get Back Together	Verbalize acceptance that parents will not reunite	7-10	I,G
Sometimes My Parent Misses Visits	Verbalize feelings re: parent missing visits	7-12	I
I Am Angry at My Parent	Verbalize positive feelings toward both parents	9-12	I
Billy's Story	Verbalize positive feelings toward both parents	8-12	I
There Was Violence in My Family	Verbalize feelings regarding family violence	7-12	I
I Don't See My Parent Anymore	Verbalize feelings of estrangement from parent	7-12	I
My Parents are Dating	Verbalize feelings regarding dating	7-12	I,G
My Parents are Getting Remarried	Verbalize feelings regarding remarriage	7-12	I,G
Basketball Game about Divorce	Verbalize an understanding of divorce	7-12	I
Ali and Her Mixed-Up Feelings Jar	Identify and express feelings related to divorce	7-10	I,G
My Body Doesn't Feel Good	Decrease frequency of somatic complaints	7-10	I,G
Feeling Sad	Identify and express feelings of sadness	7-12	I,G
Feeling Angry	Express anger through appropriate outlets	7-12	I,G
Feeling Like It's My Fault	Eliminate self-blame statements regarding divorce	8-12	I
Getting Rid Of Guilt	Eliminate self-blame statements regarding divorce	8-12	I
Getting Into Trouble	Identify feelings, reduce acting out behavior	8-12	I
Heads or Tails Feelings Game	Identify and express feelings related to divorce	7-12	I
Feeling Good About Myself	Identify positive traits about self	7-12	I,G
Coping with Bad Dreams	Implement adaptive coping techniques	7-10	I,G
I Deserve To Be Happy	Verbalize positive thoughts about future	7-12	I,G
I Can Have a Happy Marriage	Verbalize positive thoughts regarding marriage	7-10	I,G
Feel Good Messages	Implement adaptive coping techniques	7-12	I,G
Coping with Divorce Game	Implement adaptive coping techniques	7-12	I,G
What I Learned	Review therapeutic gains	7-12	I
Giving a Helping Hand	Articulate helpful message to other children	7-12	I,G
Balloon Bounce	Establish group rapport	7+	G
Scavenger Hunt	Express thoughts and feelings regarding divorce	7-12	G
Group Card Game	Express thoughts and feelings regarding divorce	7-12	G
Paper Plate Puppet Shows	Express and cope with feelings regarding divorce	7-12	G
Pizza Party	Review therapeutic gains, provide positive termination	7-12	G
Family Gift	Assess family dynamics	All	F
Family Card Game	Increase communication in family	7+	F
Typical Day	Establish and abide by rules and routines	7-10	F
Postcards	Identify needs to parents	8-12	F
Play Date	Parents spend one-on-one time with child	7-12	F
Nightly Snuggle	Parents provide child with nurturance	6-12	F

Modality: I= Individual Therapy, G= Group Therapy, F=Family Therapy

Section 1

GUIDELINES FOR PRACTITIONERS

Have a Strong Theoretical Foundation

Practitioners should be well-grounded in their theoretical orientation before using any activities or techniques in therapy sessions with children. Interventions should not be used indiscriminately or in a manner that ignores clinical theory. The activities in this book can be integrated into any theoretical orientation that uses a directive child therapy approach.

Be Well-Informed in Child Language Acquisition

Many of the activities in this book depend on language as the primary means of communication, and require the child to have language mastery. The practitioner must, therefore, be well-informed in child language acquisition, and only use the activities in this book with children who have the capacity to comprehend the activities and, where needed, verbalize their thoughts and feelings.

Use Interventions that are Appropriate for Each Client

There are a variety of interventions to choose from in this book. The child's developmental capacities should be considered to ensure that the selected activity is age-appropriate. (The *Activities at a Glance* has been included to guide the practitioner in this regard.) The child's interests should also be considered so the activity appeals to him or her and sustains his or her motivation. Select activities to fit the child's treatment goals. Pacing is also important. Consider the child's level of engagement in therapy and degree of defensiveness before implementing activities that are more emotionally intense, or that require the child to take greater emotional risk. The therapist should also moderate emotionally-laden material with more neutral experiences.

Meet with the Parents Prior to Seeing the Child

It is recommended to meet with the parents prior to seeing the child. This allows the practitioner to engage the parents and obtain information for the assessment. If possible, meet with both parents together, unless there are safety concerns that prohibit the parties from coming into contact. It can still be beneficial to conduct a joint session when there is a high level of conflict between the parents, as this can provide valuable assessment information and set the tone for working collaboratively with both parents. It can also be helpful to observe each parent separately with the child. (The intervention, *Family Gift*, in Section Nine can be used as part of the parent-child observation sessions.)

Confirm Custody and Obtain Consents from Both Parents

Although the focus of the first session with the parents is on rapport building and information gathering, there are a number of important administrative tasks that need to be accomplished. A copy of the divorce papers should be obtained in order to confirm custody. Written consent to treatment should be obtained from both custodial parents. In cases of sole custody, it is clinically beneficial to obtain consent to treatment from the non-custodial parent, in order to encourage this parent's involvement in therapy and secure support for the child's therapy.

Remain Neutral

Both parents may strive to win the practitioner's allegiance. In some cases, they will try to influence the practitioner to view one parent as the good parent, and the other as the bad one. One parent may blame the child's problems on the other parent, not acknowledging responsibility for his or her contribution to any unhealthy dynamics. In order to be most effective, the practitioner must not become aligned with one parent or get drawn into the conflict. The practitioner should take a neutral stance with the parents and remain focused on the needs of the child. The practitioner can maintain neutrality with parents while still conveying empathy for their pain and respect for their points of view. Neutrality is important because of the dichotomous thinking that is common in divorced families. Parents engaged in high levels of conflict will need ongoing help from the therapist to disengage from the dispute and to focus on plans and rules of conduct for the future.

Obtain a Signed Custody/Access Dispute Contract

In some cases, divorced parents who seek therapy for their children have a hidden agenda to use the therapy information in legal proceedings. It is not the role of the child therapist to conduct a custody and access assessment, or to make recommendations to the court. The child therapist should avoid becoming involved in the custody proceedings. It is therefore strongly recommended that both parents be asked to sign a *Custody/Access Dispute Contract* before proceeding with any clinical assessment or treatment. (See Appendix.) While this contract is not legally binding, it is clinically beneficial to have this document signed by both parents.

Develop a Therapeutic Rapport

Regardless of the activity being used, the therapist-client relationship is central to the client's realization of treatment goals. Since the rapport that develops between therapist and child forms the foundation for therapeutic success, the practitioner must create an atmosphere of safety in which the child is made to feel accepted, understood, and respected.

Conduct an Assessment and Develop a Treatment Plan

The clinical assessment is a critical component of the intervention process, as it is the basis for effective treatment planning. Therefore, the assessment interventions in Section Four should be completed prior to using any of the treatment interventions. These assessment activities can be combined with additional assessment information, family interviews, collateral reports, and diagnostic measures to evaluate the child and his or her family, and to formulate a treatment plan.

The treatment plan should set realistic, measurable goals, and be revised as needed. The treatment plan should be evaluated at appropriate intervals with parents, the treatment team, and (if appropriate) with the child. A sample *Treatment Plan* is included in the Appendix.

Once the assessment is completed, a meeting with the parents should take place to provide feedback on the assessment, consider treatment recommendations, and contract for service.

Understand the Difference between Clarification and Correction

During the assessment phase, the goal is to *clarify* the child's perceptions about self, others, and the world. For example, in an assessment activity, if the child says, "The divorce was my fault," an appropriate clarification response from the practitioner would be, "Tell me why you think it is your fault." During the treatment phase, the goal shifts to doing *corrective* work, or challenging the child's cognitive distortions.

Involve the Parents in Treatment

Children's healthy adjustment to divorce depends largely on how well the parents handle the situation. Parents should, therefore, be a part of treatment. Sessions can be conducted with the child and each of his or her parents separately to enhance the parent-child relationship and facilitate optimal communication. Section Nine contains interventions for family sessions. If parents are engaged in ongoing conflict, the child therapist can refer them to appropriate resources, such as divorce mediation, or a parenting coordinator.

Give Each Child a Scrapbook

It is recommended that the child be given a scrapbook in the first session in which to place activities completed during sessions. The scrapbook has *several* benefits: it allows the child to see the progression of sessions; it provides immediate, tangible reinforcement of each therapeutic success; and it gives the child a lasting record once therapy is terminated.

All therapeutic activities completed by the child during sessions should be placed in the scrapbook, and it should be kept in a locked place in the practitioner's office. It can be given to the child in his or her last session, with a discussion regarding who, if anyone, should see it, and where in the child's home it should be kept to ensure its privacy. (A complete copy of the scrapbook must be made for the practitioner's file prior to giving it to the child.) For further information about the use of therapeutic scrapbooks, refer to the article, *The Resolution Scrapbook as an Aid in the Treatment of Traumatized Children,* published in the <u>Journal of Child Welfare</u>, July 1995 (this article can also be found on the author's web page: <u>www.lianalowenstein.com</u>).

Give Each Child a Feel Better Bag

Encouraging self-care and teaching healthy coping strategies is important to do with clients. It is particularly crucial for children dealing with divorce, since their parents may be consumed with their own stress and may not be able to meet the child's emotional needs. It is also important to teach coping skills at the beginning of the intervention process, so clients can master these skills prior to facing anxiety-provoking material during treatment. The *Feel Better Bag* is used as a tool to facilitate self-care. This bag is given to the child in the first session to take home, and in subsequent sessions the child is provided with a self-care item to add to the bag. Ideas for the *Feel Better Bag* are incorporated throughout this book. The practitioner should ask the child at the beginning of each session whether s/he used the *Feel Better Bag* and, if so, whether it was helpful.

Maintain a Consistent Structure to Sessions

Each session should adhere to a similar structure, so the child knows what to expect. It can be helpful to begin each session with a check-in ritual to assess current functioning and facilitate self-expression. For example, the client can be asked to rate his or her week on a scale of one to ten (one being terrible and ten being perfect), or draw a feeling face to show how s/he feels. The client can also be asked if s/he used a strategy from the *Feel Better Bag* and how it helped him or her to cope better. A quick engagement activity can then be played, such as *Feelings Tic-Tac-Toe* (see Section Four). Next, the child can complete the activity or activities planned for the session (although the practitioner should be prepared to divert from the planned activity if needed). The child can then choose an activity to do, such as a board game, craft, or playing with toys in the room. Some children will need a more energetic activity at the end of the session to appropriately channel excess adrenalin caused by anxiety. As mentioned above, all completed activities should be placed in the child's scrapbook, and the child should be provided with something to take home to add to his or her *Feel Better Bag*.

Be Well-Prepared in Advance of Sessions

Before using any assessment or treatment exercise, the practitioner should first review the activity and gather any necessary materials. If the practitioner lacks confidence, then practicing and rehearsing the activity with a colleague before the session may be helpful. However, no matter how well-prepared the practitioner is for the session, the unforeseen can happen. The practitioner, therefore, needs to be flexible and modify the plan according to the child's needs.

Introduce, Process, and Bring Closure to Each Activity

When implementing an activity, first consider how it will be introduced to the child. The therapist's enthusiasm, creativity, and overall style will be key factors in determining if the child will become interested and engaged in the activity. All activities should be carefully processed and used as a point of departure for further discussion. The practitioner can encourage the child to elaborate by asking open-ended questions such as, "Tell me more about that," or by inquiring about a particular detail of the child's work. As the child moves to a more engaged and ready state, deeper issues can be skillfully explored and processed. When the activity has been completed and sufficiently processed, the therapist should provide positive feedback to the child on his or her completed work and bring closure to the activity.

Set Appropriate Limits

Children in therapy may test limits, often because they feel overwhelmed by the divorce and other life stressors, and lack the capacity to handle their strong emotions. It is important to provide the child with limits and structure. Practitioners must be consistent when setting limits, but take care not to jeopardize the therapeutic rapport. Suggestions for managing challenging client behaviors can be found in the author's book, *More Creative Interventions for Troubled Children and Youth.*

Provide a Positive Termination Experience

The termination phase of treatment must be handled with sensitivity, particularly with children of divorce who may experience the end of therapy as another loss. During this phase, the child may experience feelings of sadness, anger, rejection, and abandonment. Termination can also be a wonderfully positive experience as the child's therapeutic progress and achievements are highlighted and celebrated.

A graduation ceremony can be planned for the last session with the child, to help create a positive, celebratory atmosphere for this important phase of intervention. The practitioner can write a letter to present to the child at the graduation ceremony. This letter will review goals achieved in therapy, validate the child's efforts and accomplishments, reinforce healthy thoughts, and provide a positive message for the child's future (see Appendix for a sample letter). The letter can be placed at the end of the child's scrapbook.

Obtain Professional and Personal Support

Working with families of divorce can be professionally and emotionally challenging. It is, therefore, important to obtain good clinical supervision from a supervisor who is knowledgeable in treating families of divorce. Clinical supervision can help the therapist maintain a working alliance with both parents, and maintain balance in the face of parents' demands for allegiance. It is also important for practitioners to make use of support from colleagues and friends, and engage in regular self-care rituals.

Section 2

Children of Divorce: A Brief Theoretical Overview

Clinicians using this book should be well-trained in issues specific to separation and divorce. Below is a brief theoretical overview. Suggestions for additional reading can be found in the *References and Suggested Readings* section in the Appendix.

Stages of Divorce

According to Wallerstein and Blakeslee (1989), there are three stages of divorce, though some families get stuck in one stage, rather than progressing through all three stages.

The first stage is the increasing marital conflict that results in one parent initiating the marital separation. This stage is marked by chaos and disorganization in the family. Children are often exposed to anger and sometimes physical violence between their parents. They may become aware of a parent getting involved in other sexual relationships. Parents in this stage are usually preoccupied, so daily routines and consistent parenting may be disrupted. Children need more attention and stability at this time, yet they usually get less.

Stage two is a transitional one. It is during this stage that families attempt to reorganize and rebuild their lives in new ways. Adults may return to school or get new jobs, move to another home, or begin dating. Children often change schools, and make new friends. Family life is still somewhat unstable, but attempts at rebuilding are being made.

In the third stage, the family has reached a fairly stable equilibrium. Visitation and child support agreements have been settled. Living and school arrangements have been established. However, this family is still more vulnerable to stressors than before the marital separation. This is because there are more financial pressures, less support during emergencies, and more stresses placed on the single-parent household. If either parent remarries, then a new period of instability occurs.

Impact of Divorce on Children at Different Developmental Stages

Regardless of their age, all children are affected by parental breakup. The chart on the next page summarizes children's responses to separation and divorce at different developmental stages. Effective practice with children of divorce is best achieved by understanding this developmental context. Development is an individual process that proceeds generally as outlined in the chart, but variations may occur. Moreover, the chart is a general summary and cannot include all possible reactions.

Impact of Divorce on Children at Different Developmental Stages
(Adapted from Johnston & Roseby, 1997; Solomon, 2005)

Age	Characteristics	Separation issues	Signs of distress	Suggestions
0-8 months	-Dependent on parents for meeting their needs -Develop trust through consistent care-giving	-Continue to meet basic needs after separation. As long as needs are met, sleep environment not critical	-Sleep disturbance -Clinginess -Crying	-Opportunities to bond with both parents -Physical comfort -Consistent routine
8 months-2 years	-Form attachments to caregivers between 8-18 months	-Will feel loss of primary caregivers. Keep stasis as much as possible	-Same as above	-Do not make major changes to routine, sleep situation, caregiver -Physical comfort
2-4	-Developing more independence -Verbal skills develop to express feelings and needs -Can keep absent parent in mind to comfort self	-May experience loss of contact with parent as abandonment -May have sense of responsibility for separation -Anxious about needs being met (food, shelter, visitation)	-Regression (lapses in toilet training, returning to security blanket or old toys) -Anxiety at bedtime -Fear abandonment -Seek physical contact -Irritable, tantrums	-Physical comfort -Consistent routine -Allow some regression -Will adapt to longer separations from one parent through frequent visits with the other parent
5-8	-Developing peer relationships -Moral development progresses	-May feel responsible for the separation -Fantasies of parental reunification -Fear abandonment, long for absent parent	-Overt signs of grief such as sadness, anger -Feelings of abandonment and rejection -Changes in eating and sleeping -Behavioral problems -Loyalty conflicts -May try to take on role of departing parent	-Opportunities to express feelings, learn coping strategies -Reassurance that they are not responsible for the separation -Permission to love both parents -Participation in extracurricular activities to detach from parental problems -Benefit from spending as much time as possible with each parent
9-12	-Increased awareness of self -Trying to fit in with peers	-Angry about the separation -May feel responsible for the separation -Likely to take sides, blame parent they think caused the separation -May make one parent all good and the other all bad	-Intense anger -Physical complaints -Overactive to avoid thinking about separation -Feel ashamed about separation, feel different from other children -More likely to ally with a parent or be alienated	-Opportunities to express feelings -Learn skills to cope -Reassurance they are not responsible for separation -Permission to love both parents -Participation in extracurricular activities to detach from parental problems -Benefit from spending as much time as possible with each parent
13-18	-Solidifying identity and establishing self in relation to rules and regulations of society	-May feel embarrassed by family break-up and react by de-idealizing one or both parents -Place peer needs ahead of family and may not want to visit non-resident parent	-Withdrawal from family -Difficulty concentrating -Engaging in high-risk behaviors (sexual promiscuity, drug and alcohol use) -Worry about own future relationships	-Consistent limits balanced with more freedom and choices -Have input about visitation but not burdened by having to decide custody & access schedule

Intervention that is timely and effective can have an important positive impact on a child's subsequent development. The child's relationship with his or her family, experiences in school and with peers, and ongoing life events will have much more cumulative influence on a child's development than will professional intervention. However, timely intervention can help a child shift away from an unhealthy pathway and onto a more adaptive one that has long-term implications for development.

Children's Adjustment to Separation and Divorce

Most children experience considerable distress in the early stages of divorce. Common reactions include sadness, anxiety, anger, guilt, confusion, loyalty conflicts, and yearning for the absent parent. Research has shown that children of divorce are at greater risk of depression, behavioral problems, and school difficulties (Clulow, 1990; Hetherington, Stanley-Hagan, & Anderson, 1989; Oppawsky, 1991; Pedro-Carroll, 2001). Studies have also shown that self-blame and misconceptions about the divorce can lead to more difficulties for children (Kurdek & Berg, 1983, 1987). Interventions that clarify misconceptions and provide accurate attributions for parental problems can help school-aged children adjust better (Alpert-Gillis, Pedro-Carroll, & Cowen, 1989; Pedro-Carroll, Sutton, & Wyman, 1999; Stolberg & Mahler, 1994). Enhancing coping abilities, particularly problem-solving and positive thinking, contributes to resilience among children (Sandler, Tein, Mehta, Wolchik, & Ayers, 2000). This research speaks to the need for intervention to focus on strengthening the child's coping strategies.

Some children may become psychologically scarred from the divorce, whereas others may come out of it relatively unscathed. Much depends on how well the parents handle the situation. Kelly and Emery (2003) note the following factors that facilitate children's healthy adjustment to divorce:

- Good adjustment of residential parent
- Competent parenting
- Regular access with adequate non-residential parent
- Reduced and encapsulated conflict between parents
- Parallel or cooperative co-parenting arrangements
- Limited family transitions

There are a number of important clinical implications that derive from the above summary of children's adjustment to separation and divorce. As Kelly states, "Whatever its specific nature or focus, interventions are more likely to benefit children from divorced families if they seek to contain parental conflict, promote authoritative and close relationships between children and both of their parents, enhance economic stability in the post-divorce family, and, when appropriate, involve children in effective interventions that help them have a voice in shaping more individualized and helpful access arrangements" (2002).

Intervention should not merely be provided for the child, but should also involve the parents. Intervention for parents should focus on divorce education, reducing parental conflict, enhancing parenting, and facilitating an appropriate parenting plan. The child therapist should encourage parents to make use of available resources that can provide these interventions, such as parent education programs, divorce mediation, parenting coordinators, collaborative lawyering, judicial settlement conferences, and family and group therapy for children and parents (Kelly 2002).

Psychological Tasks

According to Wallerstein (1983), children of divorce must master six interrelated, hierarchical psychological tasks. The first three are acknowledging the reality of the marital rupture, disengaging from parental conflict, and pursuing customary activities within one year of the initial separation. It is only after these three tasks have been successfully accomplished that children can proceed with the other tasks, which are mastered over a period of many years. These involve resolving feelings related to the partial or total loss of a parent from the family unit, working through feelings of anger and guilt, and accepting the permanence of the divorce. During adolescence or young adulthood, the final task must be mastered, that of achieving realistic hope about their own intimate relationships.

The activities in this book have been developed with the above tasks in mind, in order to facilitate the therapeutic process for children dealing with separation and divorce.

Continuum of Child-Parent Relationships after Divorce

According to Kelly and Johnston (2001), children's relationships to each parent following separation and divorce can be conceptualized along a continuum from positive to negative (with the most negative being the alienated child) as described below:

Positive relationship with both parents: At the most healthy end of the continuum are children who have a positive relationship with both parents and wish to spend significant amounts of time with each parent.

Affinity with one parent: Also at the healthy end of the continuum are children who are closer emotionally to one parent. Due to gender, age, temperament, shared interests, and parenting practices, these children feel much closer to one parent, but still want substantial contact with and love from both parents.

Allied children: Further along the continuum are children who are aligned with one parent. They have an exaggerated connection with that parent and express ambivalent feelings toward the non-preferred parent. They typically want limited contact with the non-preferred parent after the marital separation. This alliance may stem from intense marital conflict in which the child was encouraged to take sides. Or the child is unable to tolerate the tension surrounding the highly conflicted divorce and opts out of the unbearable conflict by choosing to be aligned with one parent while avoiding the other parent. The child is most likely to align with the parent who s/he perceives to have the most power, or the one s/he believes is more hurt or vulnerable.

Estranged children: These are children who are realistically estranged from one parent due to that parent's history of family violence, abuse, neglect, or severe parental deficiencies, such as substance abuse, psychiatric disorders, or an angry and rigid parenting style. It is a healthy response when the child distances himself from a parent who is consistently inadequate or abusive. The anger and fear the child has toward this parent is appropriate and should be processed in therapy. If the child was abused or witnessed domestic violence, this trauma should be assessed and treated. Deficient or abusive parents clearly need therapeutic intervention but, unfortunately, they often deny their parenting deficiencies and accuse the other parent of making false allegations against them.

<u>Alienated children</u>: At the far end of the continuum are children who are alienated from a parent after separation or divorce, who express their rejection of that parent without ambivalence, and who strongly resist or refuse contact with that rejected parent. These rejected parents have no *severe* parenting deficiencies and have not been abusive so the child's negative views toward them are significantly distorted and unrealistic. Johnston (2003) concludes that alienation is caused by multiple systemic factors, including the aligned parent's denigration of the rejected parent, the rejected parent's lack of empathy and support for the aligned child, and harsh/rigid parenting style. Alienated children are generally more troubled, dependent, less socially competent, have low self-esteem, poor reality testing, lack the capacity for ambivalence, and are prone to enmeshment or splitting in relations with others (Johnston & Roseby, 1997; Kelly & Johnston, 2001; Warshak, 2001, 2003). In order to intervene appropriately, one must understand the roots of the alienation. According to Warshak, "Relief from alienation requires an understanding of all the contributing factors. The child may have [his or her] own motives, the rejected parent may be responding in a rigid manner that reinforces the negative attitudes, and the favored parent may be actively or passively supporting the rupture of the parent-child relationship." (2002, p. 49).

Therapeutic intervention for families with alienation should focus on transforming the child's distorted "good/bad" views of his or her parents into more realistic ones, and restoring appropriate parent-child relationships and co-parental roles in the family. Intervention should include the child, siblings, and the aligned and rejected parent, and other family members (Johnston, Walters, and Friedlander, 2001).

The child therapist must not become involved in the unhealthy dynamics of child alienation cases. He or she should not support the child's distorted views of the rejected parent or become aligned with either parent. It is not the role of the child therapist to make decisions about parenting schedules or co-parenting issues. Rather, the therapist's role is to help the child adjust to the divorce and to treat the dynamics of the child's alienation (Sullivan and Kelly, 2001). Because understanding and intervening with the alienated child is particularly complicated, practitioners are strongly urged to obtain specialized training and familiarize themselves with current literature on the topic before intervening with this client population.

Cases are often mismanaged when children are inappropriately labeled alienated when, in fact, their resistance toward contact with a parent is due to normal, expectable reasons, including estrangement. When a child strongly and consistently resists contact with a parent, a comprehensive assessment is required to determine if s/he is aligned, estranged, or alienated (Kelly and Johnson, 2001). This assessment should be court-ordered and conducted by a neutral evaluator who has knowledge and skill in this area. The results of the assessment should be shared with all legal and mental health professionals who will be involved with the family, and interventions should be provided by a collaborative team who have expertise in working with divorced families.

Section 3

Meeting with Parents

It is recommended that the parents be interviewed, preferably together, prior to meeting the child. The focus of this initial session is on establishing a positive rapport with each parent, explaining the therapeutic process, completing administrative forms, and learning about the child and family. Although the focus should be on the child's issues, each parent can be given an opportunity to vent. Parents will be better able to focus on their child if they have been given the opportunity to voice their own concerns. However, some limits must be placed on this venting, and the interview redirected to the needs of the child. If a parent has difficulty shifting focus away from the marital conflict and onto the child, the practitioner can ask the parent to put his or her concerns in writing after the session.

Some parents may refuse to meet with the child's therapist. This may be due to the parent's perception that the therapist is aligned with the other parent, or the fear that he or she will be negatively judged. In this situation, the practitioner must make every effort to engage the parent and communicate neutrality. One strategy is for the practitioner to communicate to the parent (in a caring tone) that the child's therapy will be seriously hindered without the participation of both parents.

Interventions

Letter: The letter (see following sample) can be given to parents in the initial session. It covers information about the therapist's role and the therapeutic process. When working with cases of divorce, it can be helpful to set some ground rules with the parents in order to preempt potential problems. The letter to the parents outlines these ground rules.

Questionnaire: Detailed information should be obtained from each parent and other primary caregivers as part of the assessment process. The questionnaire collects the following information:

- The child's current living arrangements
- The child's developmental history
- The child's current difficulties
- Circumstances of the marital separation
- Reactions to the family breakup
- Family information
- Parent history

The information on the questionnaire should be collected via a face-to-face interview with each parent. This facilitates rapport-building, and allows the practitioner to elicit richer diagnostic information than would otherwise be obtained if the parents were to complete it on their own. During the interview, it is important to give each parent equal opportunity to share information about themselves and the child. In addition to the content gathered on the questionnaire, the parent session can provide the practitioner with other useful assessment information, including the parents' ability to take some responsibility for the marital conflict, each parent's level of anger toward the other parent, their insight into the child's needs, and their ability to support a co-parenting arrangement.

Handout: The handout, *Helping Your Child through Separation and Divorce,* provides parents with information about children and divorce. The hope is that this information will better equip parents to respond to the special needs of their children. The handout can be given to parents to read on their own. However, it will be more useful to review the handout in parent sessions, and to discuss how each parent can shift his or her behavior to create a healthier environment for the child.

Letter to Parent

Dear Parent,

I have prepared this letter to provide you with some information about my role, the therapeutic process, and what to expect from therapy. It is my hope that this information will help us work together so we can be a supportive team for your child. My role is to provide a safe therapeutic environment in which your child can openly express his or her thoughts and feelings. Since children typically have difficulty talking about their issues, I use play-based activities, such as therapeutic games and art, to make it easier for them to share their feelings. I will begin by completing an assessment on your child. The information that you provide to me will be an important part of this assessment. I may also request to meet with your family as part of the assessment, as this can help me develop a better understanding of your child's needs. Once I have completed my assessment, I will provide you with feedback and make recommendations.

The goal of therapy is to help children deal with the divorce and other stresses in a healthy way. This involves helping children face their difficulties a little at a time, and teaching them skills to cope with their difficulties. Each child is unique and requires a treatment plan geared especially to his or her needs. We will work together to develop realistic treatment goals.

As therapy progresses, you may notice some changes in your child's behaviors and symptoms. For example, your child may experience an increase in some of the following: nightmares, fears, aggression, tantrums, or difficulties concentrating. This is normal as your child begins to confront his or her difficulties. If this becomes a concern, please do not hesitate to set up a session with me so we can discuss how to best support you and your child during this difficult time.

It is important that you bring your child to therapy as scheduled and on time. Children feel more secure and do better in therapy when they have consistent appointments. Please do not talk about concerns regarding your child to me in front of your child. This usually makes children feel uncomfortable. If you would like to discuss a concern, please call me prior to the session. Please ensure your child cannot hear the phone conversation. Many children find it uncomfortable when their parents ask them to talk about details of their sessions. It is helpful to ask your child a more general question, such as, "How was your session today?" The child can then decide what he or she feels like sharing. I certainly understand your concern and interest in your child's therapy, and we will meet regularly to discuss your child's progress.

Divorce is stressful for all family members. There may be times when you wish to speak to me about a concern you have about the other parent. However, in order for me to be most helpful to your family, it is imperative that I not get involved in any conflict between you and the other parent. Therefore, please refrain from discussing the other parent with me, unless it pertains to the needs of your child. If you are concerned about your child's safety, please contact your local child welfare agency. Please note that I am obligated by law to report any safety concerns to proper authorities. In order for your child to view me as a support and not as a detective or assessor, it is important that I not be involved in any custody proceedings. I will therefore request that you sign a Custody/Access Dispute Contract.

Children's adjustment to divorce depends largely on how well parents handle the situation. I have, therefore, prepared a handout with some helpful tips for you to read. It is also important to know that your child will do better if you are involved in the therapy. We will discuss this further so we can come up with a plan that makes sense for both you and your child. I look forward to working with your child and family.

Sincerely,

(Signature of Therapist)

Questionnaire for Parents

Child's Name: _____ Date of Birth: _____ Address: _____
Mother's Name: _____ Date of Birth: _____ Occupation: _____
Father's Name: _____ Date of Birth: _____ Occupation: _____
Home Phone #: _____ Mother's Work/Cell #: _____ Father's Work/Cell #: _____
Child's School: _____ Teacher: _____ Grade: _____ Phone #: _____
Who has legal custody of the child? _____ (Please provide copy of custody order for the file)

List all those living in child's home:

Name	Relationship	Age/School/Occupation

List other persons closely involved with child but not living in the home:
_____
_____

What are your concerns about your child that made you bring him/her to therapy?
_____
_____
_____

List any complications at birth and delays in development or difficulties when child was an infant/toddler:
_____
_____
_____
_____

List any ongoing health concerns/allergies/medications child is taking and describe for what purpose:
_____
_____

Describe any serious difficulties or life stresses child has experienced, other than the separation/divorce:
_____
_____
_____
_____
_____

Describe prior assessment/therapy child received (Name of professional, date of service, diagnosis):
_____
_____

Describe your relationship with child's other biological parent prior to separation (when and how you met, length of courtship, date of marriage, positive and negative aspects of your relationship):
_____
_____
_____

Circumstances of marital separation (date of separation, who initiated and why, current feelings toward other biological parent):

_____
_____
_____

When and how did you explain the reason for the separation to the child?

_____
_____

Describe child's reaction to the marital separation immediately afterward, and since the separation:

_____
_____
_____

What is the current legal status? (Custody, visitation arrangements, upcoming court dates):

_____
_____

Please describe any ongoing conflict between you and the other biological parent:

_____
_____
_____

Are you or the other biological parent presently dating? Please elaborate and describe child's reaction:

_____
_____

Have there been any other major changes in the home situation, i.e. moved, parent's work schedule, etc.?

_____
_____

Describe your relationship with your child, and your strengths and weaknesses as a parent:

_____
_____
_____
_____

Describe the other parent's relationship with the child, and his or her strengths and weaknesses as a parent:

_____
_____
_____
_____

What role do you see the other biological parent playing in the child's life?

_____
_____

Describe any concerns about your family (health, mental illness, alcohol/drug dependency, abuse):

_____
_____
_____
_____
_____

Please describe any concerns about your child listed below:

Difficulty sleeping/frequent nightmares: _____

Bed-wetting or soiling: _____

Unusually clingy or immature behavior: _____

Excessive fears, anxiety: _____

Physical complaints (stomachaches, headaches): _____

Change in eating habits: _____

Little sense of joy/happiness: _____

Hurts self on purpose/talks of wanting to die: _____

Blatant misbehavior: _____

Aggressive with others: _____

Hurts animals on purpose: _____

Sets fires: _____

Lies/steals: _____

Hides food: _____

School difficulties: _____

Difficulties with peers: _____

Inappropriate sexual behavior: _____

Poor self-esteem: _____

Please describe any other concerns you have about your child:

_____

_____

_____

_____

_____

_____

What are your child's strengths and interests?

_____

_____

_____

_____

Would you give permission for your child to receive food or candy during sessions? Yes___ No___

Mother's Background:

Where were you raised and by whom? Describe past/current relationship with your parents:

_____
_____
_____
_____

List brothers and sisters, their ages, whereabouts, current relationship you have:

_____
_____
_____
_____

Describe any of the following you/your family experienced during childhood and how it affected you (physical/sexual abuse, neglect, abandonment, spousal abuse, divorce, other trauma):

_____
_____
_____
_____

How were you disciplined and by whom?

_____
_____

Describe your parents' relationship, and how they resolved conflict, i.e. reasoning, withdrawing, yelling, hitting:

_____
_____

Describe the happiest time/experience you recall from your childhood:

_____
_____

Describe the saddest time/experience you recall from your childhood:

_____
_____

Describe if you or any relatives have ever had any of the following:
Serious illness: _____
Depression/Bipolar Disorder: _____
Anxiety Disorder: _____
Obsessive-Compulsive Disorder: _____
Learning Disability/ADHD: _____
Eating Disorder: _____
Alcoholism/Drug Abuse: _____
Criminal Conviction: _____

Please add any other information about your background that you feel is important:

_____
_____
_____

Father's Background:

Where were you raised and by whom? Describe past/current relationship with your parents:

_____
_____
_____
_____

List brothers and sisters, their ages, whereabouts, current relationship you have:

_____
_____
_____
_____

Describe any of the following you/your family experienced during childhood and how it affected you (physical/ sexual abuse, neglect, abandonment, spousal abuse, divorce, other trauma):

_____
_____
_____
_____

How were you disciplined and by whom?

_____
_____

Describe your parents' relationship, and how they resolved conflict, i.e. reasoning, withdrawing, yelling, hitting:

_____
_____

Describe the happiest time/experience you recall from your childhood:

_____
_____

Describe the saddest time/experience you recall from your childhood:

_____
_____

Describe if you or any relatives have ever had any of the following:
Serious illness: _____
Depression/Bipolar Disorder: _____
Anxiety Disorder: _____
Obsessive-Compulsive Disorder: _____
Learning Disability/ADHD: _____
Eating Disorder: _____
Alcoholism/Drug Abuse: _____
Criminal Conviction: _____

Please add any other information about your background that you feel is important:

_____
_____
_____
_____

Background of Other Primary Caregivers (i.e. Stepparent, Common Law Partner):

Where were you raised and by whom? Describe past/current relationship with your parents:

_____
_____
_____
_____

List brothers and sisters, their ages, whereabouts, current relationship you have:

_____
_____
_____
_____

Describe any of the following you/your family experienced during childhood and how it affected you (physical/sexual abuse, neglect, abandonment, spousal abuse, divorce, other trauma):

_____
_____
_____
_____

How were you disciplined and by whom?

_____
_____

Describe your parents' relationship, and how they resolved conflict, i.e. reasoning, withdrawing, yelling, hitting:

_____
_____

Describe the happiest time/experience you recall from your childhood:

_____
_____

Describe the saddest time/experience you recall from your childhood:

_____
_____

Describe if you or any relatives have ever had any of the following:
Serious illness: _____
Depression/Bipolar Disorder: _____
Anxiety Disorder: _____
Obsessive-Compulsive Disorder: _____
Learning Disability/ADHD: _____
Eating Disorder: _____
Alcoholism/Drug Abuse: _____
Criminal Conviction: _____

Please add any other information about your background that you feel is important:

_____
_____
_____
_____

Helping Your Children through Separation and Divorce

Divorce is stressful for children, but there are things you can do to help your child during this time of change and loss.

1) Give your child a simple but honest explanation about the separation or divorce so s/he understands it was not his or her fault. If possible, no matter how painful, try to tell them when the whole family is together (including both spouses and all children).

2) Be available to listen. Accept the child's feelings (most typically sadness, anger, guilt) and remind him or her that his or her feelings and reactions are normal. Use words that invite more, such as, "Tell me more about that," or "What was that like?" Help your child be open with you by saying: "You can tell me anything and I won't be mad at you no matter what."

3) Reassure your child early and often that your divorce is not his or her fault.

4) Tell your child you love him or her. Children may believe that, because their parents stop loving each other, they may also someday stop loving their children.

5) Don't punish or reprimand immature behavior. Children of all ages who feel stressed may act babyish for awhile, i.e. baby-talking, bed-wetting, or thumb-sucking. They need extra comfort and affection during this time.

6) Set up a regular visitation schedule. Children feel most secure when they know when and for how long the visitation will occur.

7) Even if you live far away from your child, regular contact by phone, email, or via video computer is important to let your child know you care about him or her.

8) Divorce is a time of change for both you and your child. Try to minimize these changes. For example, try to keep your child in the same school and home if possible, as well as the same afternoon and evening activities.

9) Use consistent rules and routines. For example, try to agree with the other parent what TV programs are permitted, what bedtime is appropriate, how misbehavior is handled, etc. Write down and exchange this agreed-upon list of rules and routines.

10) Don't feel you need to provide special toys, treats, or outings at each visit. Children need normal family time in both parents' homes.

11) Don't argue or fight with your ex-spouse while the child is listening. Experts say the amount of conflict children witness during and after divorce is a crucial factor in their adjustment. If you are having difficulty keeping the conflict to a minimum, please get help!

12) Don't criticize your ex-spouse in front of your child. Remember that your ex-spouse is still your child's parent; when you criticize your ex-spouse, you harm your child.

13) Don't use the child as a messenger to deliver information to the other parent.

14) Don't use your child to get revenge on the other parent by denying child support or visitation.

15) Don't use your child as a spy to find out what the other parent is doing.

16) Don't make your child take sides in any dispute with the other parent. Children generally want to make both their parents happy. Don't make them choose.

17) When you and your child do talk about the other parent, be neutral and supportive of that relationship.

18) Praise your child often. Parents in the midst of divorce are often distracted and miss opportunities to acknowledge their child's positive behavior.

19) Spend special time with your child. Your child needs you more now than ever. Try to spend at least fifteen minutes a day of uninterrupted one-on-one time with your child.

20) Do not introduce your children to potential partners until you are in a serious committed relationship. It has been shown that children exposed to numerous partners of a parent have difficulty establishing lasting committed relationships as adults, as attachment issues are disturbed.

21) Take responsibility for your own behavior. You cannot change or control your ex-spouse's behavior, but you can change and control yourself.

22) Take care of yourself. The better you take care of yourself, the better you can care for your child. Reach out for all the support that is around you: relatives, friends, support groups, etc.

Section 4

Interventions to Engage and Assess Children

Each child presents his or her own unique set of emotional, cognitive, and behavioral issues. Many children have difficulty verbalizing their concerns because they are reluctant to self-disclose and are anxious about the therapeutic process. Activities that are creative and play-based can engage otherwise resistant children, and can help them to express their thoughts and feelings. This section provides a number of interventions to engage and assess children. While these activities provide useful strategies, it is the therapist's use of self that is most powerful in engaging children. The therapist's warmth, consistency, and unconditional acceptance of the child are the key ingredients to put him or her at ease and help develop a therapeutic rapport.

Rationale for Conducting a Thorough Assessment

The ultimate purpose of assessing children is to offer them treatment that is as effective and efficient as possible. A comprehensive clinical assessment should be conducted for the following reasons:

- Determines whether the child needs treatment and, if so, what needs to be treated
- Enables the practitioner to tailor treatment to the child's needs
- Provides direction on best treatment modality, i.e. individual, group, family
- Enables the practitioner to provide accurate feedback to parents on the child's needs
- It is cost effective, since it shortens the length of treatment as it enables the therapist to hone in on exactly what needs to be treated

Areas to Assess

The clinical assessment is a critical component of the intervention process, as it forms the foundation for effective treatment planning. A thorough assessment generally requires between three and six 60-minute sessions, and should examine the following:

- The child's emotional, social, and cognitive functioning before and after the separation/divorce
- The child's relationship with each parent
- The circumstances of the separation/divorce
- The child's reactions to the separation/divorce
- The child's relationships with peers and community
- Family dynamics and any ongoing marital conflict
- The parents' strengths and vulnerabilities in caring for the child
- Other major stresses in the child's life

Sources of information for the assessment include: (a) Meeting with parents (see *Questionnaire for Parents* in Section Three); (b) Information from collateral sources; (c) Individual sessions with the child; and (d) Parent-child sessions (see Section Eleven).

The Engagement and Assessment Process

This section includes engagement and assessment tools and techniques. The engagement activities precede the assessment interventions because a therapeutic rapport must be established prior to beginning the assessment.

Many children of divorce are reluctant to trust. For this reason, the practitioner must be especially careful about establishing rapport and building a trusting relationship with these clients before delving into details related to the divorce. There are a number of ways the practitioner can encourage trust and promote openness with clients. A warm, accepting, and attentive therapeutic manner is important.

Some children may be resistant to exploring issues related to the divorce. The practitioner can help the child overcome avoidance by openly discussing his or her fears and reluctance to talk about distressing material at the beginning of the assessment process. The *Welcome Letter* covers this to some extent, but the practitioner can expand on this issue.

During the assessment, control of the pace is critical. It is important to be cognizant of non-verbal signs of discomfort if a child is reluctant to speak up. Some children may be very compliant even when they are in distress. If the child does need to take a break from an assessment activity or stop talking about a particularly distressing issue, it can be helpful to switch to an activity that fosters coping, so the child does not feel helpless. It is important to make a statement about coming back to the activity or issue at some later time when the child feels ready. This conveys the message that avoidance of distressing events is not a healthy long-term coping strategy.

During the assessment, maintaining a calm and accepting manner during the assessment will help the child feel supported. Normalizing, validating, and reflecting the child's feelings will reassure the child and communicate understanding. Once the child has completed each assessment activity, it is helpful to discuss and explore the child's responses to glean additional information. Asking open-ended questions is a particularly useful strategy for eliciting richer information from the child.

After the assessment is completed, the practitioner analyzes and interprets the data that has been collected. The accuracy of the conclusions gathered from the assessment depends largely on the skills of the assessor. The practitioner must integrate and compare the information gleaned from the assessment with: (a) knowledge of normal age-appropriate developmental issues; (b) the acquired details about the child's current issues as well as past histories; and (c) the information regarding the child gathered from other sources. The information gathered from the assessment is used to make recommendations for intervention and, where appropriate, suggestions for further assessment.

Engagement Interventions

The Welcome Letter: The initial session with the child should focus on rapport building. The child can be provided with his or her scrapbook, and the *Welcome Letter* can be placed on the first page. This letter can be read to the child to engage him or her, normalize feelings, clarify the therapist's role and duty to report safety concerns, and explain basic rules and the format of sessions. The letter can be modified for group counseling, i.e. the purpose of the group, the role of the group leaders, and group rules.

The Feel Better Bag: The child can be given the *Feel Better Bag* in the first session. The purpose of the *Feel Better Bag* is to encourage self-care and to teach healthy coping strategies. This is particularly important for children who have limited social support. It is helpful to teach the child some coping strategies early in the intervention process so s/he can use these strategies if s/he becomes anxious during a session or at home. The child can be provided with something to take home to add to the *Feel Better Bag* at the end of each session. The therapist should discuss with the child how and when to use the items in the bag. In order to encourage the child to use the *Feel Better Bag*, it is recommended that the child's parent(s) coach the child on its use at home. In addition, the practitioner should ask the child at the beginning of each session whether s/he used the *Feel Better Bag*, and whether it was helpful.

About Me/Getting to Know Each Other: These are appropriate interventions to use in initial sessions as they engage the child and help to develop rapport. Playing the *Getting to Know Each Other Potato Chip Game* helps to break through the child's resistance and facilitates open communication.

Assessment Interventions

Feeling Faces Cut 'N Paste: This activity facilitates the identification and expression of feelings. It normalizes feelings associated with divorce, and teaches feeling words to enhance the child's vocabulary. Modify for older children by having them draw feeling faces, then writing about their feelings.

Feelings Tic-Tac-Toe: Most children are familiar with *Tic-Tac-Toe* and will enjoy this version of the game. As the child talks about his or her feelings, the practitioner can reflect the child's feelings, ask the child to elaborate, and praise the child for his or her openness. When it is the practitioner's turn to share, the practitioner should tailor his or her own responses in a way that would be therapeutically beneficial to the child. *Feelings Tic-Tac-Toe* can also be played at the beginning of each session to reengage the child and quickly assess any pressing issues.

My Parents Divorce: The Dice Game: This activity ascertains the child's thoughts and feelings regarding the divorce. The game format makes the child feel more comfortable and will help the child begin talking about the divorce.

How I Think, Feel, and Behave: This activity provides rich assessment information regarding the child's emotional and behavioral reactions, as well as their intensity. Several statements on the worksheet pertain specifically to trauma symptoms, and therefore assess whether the child is suffering from emotional trauma. This activity allows children to identify their clinical issues without having to verbalize them directly, and so it is particularly useful with children who have difficulty talking directly about their problems. The practitioner should wait until the child has finished placing the self-adhesive dots on the worksheet before asking the child about his or her responses, so as to not affect the processing phase.

Butterflies in My Stomach: This activity assesses presenting problems, as well as problem-solving skills, coping abilities, and available supports. It is particularly useful with children who have a multitude of presenting problems, as it enables children to communicate to the therapist which problems are most pressing and need priority treatment.

People in My World: As part of the assessment, it is important to assess family and community relationships and available support networks. It is also important to evaluate feelings such as sadness, anger, fear, and self-blame. The practitioner can prompt the child to include self and significant family and community members on the worksheet so that these relationships can be assessed. Both positive and negative relationships should be included. If the child is reluctant to include negative relationships, the therapist can say, "It is important that you include people who have made you feel sad, scared, or angry, so you can talk about these feelings." The stickers are a useful tool to engage children in the activity. After the child has placed the stickers on the worksheet, the practitioner can ask questions to glean additional assessment information. For example, "How do you know when these people are sad/angry/scared?" and, "What do you do when these people are sad/angry/scared?"

Life's Ups & Downs: This activity assesses significant events in the child's life, and confirms that everyone has both positive and negative life experiences. In processing negative events in the child's life, the practitioner can highlight the child's resilience and coping abilities. Once the child has completed writing the events, the practitioner guides the child to discuss in more detail each memory and his or her feelings associated with each memory. It is important for the practitioner to emphasize that everyone experiences "ups and downs" in life.

Spending Time with My Mother and Father: When assessing children of divorce, it is important to evaluate the quality of the child's relationship with each parent. This activity can be used as part of a more comprehensive assessment to determine if the child has a positive relationship with each parent, or is aligned with, or alienated from, a parent. The activity can provide information about the child's closeness, safety, and comfort levels with each of his or her parents. This activity can be used as an adjunct to a family assessment to reveal dynamics in the parent-child relationship that need to be addressed in treatment.

Letter to Child

Welcome _____,
(Child's Name)

You are here today because there has been a change in your family. Your parents separated or got a divorce. A separation is when parents decide to live apart from each other and figure out what to do about their marriage. A divorce is when parents decide they no longer want to be married. They are not happy being together so they decide to stop being husband and wife. Even though your parents are separated or divorced, they are still your parents and they will always love you.

Children who are dealing with divorce usually have lots of mixed-up feelings inside. It may take a while for you to sort out these feelings and start to feel better. This is a place where you can come and talk about your feelings. You may feel nervous or scared about coming here today, but hopefully you'll feel better as we get to know each other.

My job is to listen to you and to help you through this difficult time. My job is also to help keep you safe, so if someone is hurting you, it is really important that you tell me so I can talk to the adults whose job it is to help and protect children.

To help us feel safe and okay in here, it is important that we don't hurt anybody or break anything on purpose. It is also important that the toys and materials stay in the room so they will be here when you come back next time.

Each time you come here, we will do some talking and some playing. Many children do not want to talk about upsetting things like divorce, but getting your feelings out can help you feel better. Since it can be hard to talk about divorce and painful feelings, we will use drawing activities and games to make it easier for you to share your feelings.

All your hard work will be kept in this scrapbook and it will be locked in a safe place here in the office. On your last day of coming here, you can either take your scrapbook home, or you can leave it in the office where it will be kept in a safe, private place. If you'd like, you can take some time now to decorate the cover of your scrapbook.

I look forward to talking and playing with you!

From,

_____
(Therapist's Name)

Feel Better Bag
(Supplies: Gift bag)

You have probably been feeling sad and upset since your parents' divorce, but there are things you can do to help yourself feel better. Today, you are going to get a special bag. It is called a *Feel Better Bag*. Each time you come here, you will get something to put in your *Feel Better Bag* that will help you feel better.

You can take your *Feel Better Bag* home today, and you can use it when you are feeling upset. Talk with your therapist about where to keep your *Feel Better Bag*, so you can use it when you need to.

Although this book will give you ideas of things to add to your *Feel Better Bag*, you can always add your own ideas. Remember that this special bag belongs to you, and you can use it in whatever way helps you most!

Turn the page to find out the first thing you get to put in your *Feel Better Bag*.

Something for Your Feel Better Bag:
A Hug
(Supplies: Hershey's Chocolate Hug)

Dealing with divorce can be difficult but it can help to get a hug from someone you care about, or to give yourself a hug. Put this Chocolate Hug in your *Feel Better Bag* as a reminder to hug yourself or ask for a hug when you need one.

After you have eaten your chocolate hug, keep the wrapper in your *Feel Better Bag* as a reminder that hugs can help you feel better.

About Me

Let's begin by getting to know you. Fill in these sentences:

My name is _____. I am here because my parents separated or got a divorce. My parents separated (stopped living together) when I was ____ years old. Now I am ____ years old. My favorite subject at school is _____. When I am not in school I like to _____. I am good at _____. My favorite people in my life are _____. My favorite place in the whole wide world is _____. The best thing about me is _____.

Below is a picture of me (draw a picture or glue a photo of yourself in the space below):

Something for Your Feel Better Bag:
Feel Better List

There are activities you enjoy doing, people you feel close to, and things you are good at. There are many things that make you feel better. Make a *Feel Better List* (a list of people, places, and things that make you feel better). Put your *Feel Better List* in your *Feel Better Bag*. Look at it when you feel sad as a reminder that there are people, places, and things that make you feel better.

My Feel Better List

People who make me feel better:

Places that make me feel better:

Things I do that make me feel better:

Getting to Know Each Other: The Potato Chip Game
(Supplies: Small bag of potato chips)

Getting to know each other better will help you feel more comfortable here, and make it easier for you to share your thoughts and feelings. So let's play a game to get to know each other better. It's called *The Potato Chip Game*. To play, take turns asking each other a question from the list below (or you can make up your own questions). If a player answers the question, he or she gets a potato chip. If the player does not answer the question, the other player gets the potato chip. Continue the game until you have asked each other all the questions. Remember, you get a potato chip for every question you answer!

1) What's something you like doing?
Me: _____
My Therapist: _____

2) What's your favorite color?
Me: _____
My Therapist: _____

3) What's one of your favorite foods?
Me: _____
My Therapist: _____

4) What's one of your favorite movies?
Me: _____
My Therapist: _____

5) What's something that really bugs you?
Me: _____
My Therapist: _____

6) What's one of the best things you ever did?
Me: _____
My Therapist: _____

Something for Your Feel Better Bag:
My Therapist Cares about Me

The Potato Chip Game helped you get to know your therapist. Write down some things you learned about him or her. Put your list in your *Feel Better Bag*. When you are upset, look at the list and remind yourself that this person cares about you and is there to help.

What I learned about my therapist:

Feeling Faces Cut 'N Paste
(Supplies: Scissors, glue)

Children usually have lots of feelings when their parents split up. They may feel shocked at first because they did not expect their parents to break up. They may be sad, scared, angry, nervous, or have other feelings. They may feel guilty because they blame themselves for the divorce. They may feel happy or relieved, especially if there is less fighting at home. They may have different feelings at the same time, like they may love their parents but feel angry at them for splitting up. Whatever you are feeling is a normal reaction to your parents' divorce. The *Feeling Faces Cut 'N Paste* **activity will help you talk about your feelings. Look at the feeling faces below, and cut out the ones you feel about your parents' divorce. Cut along the dotted lines. Glue them on the next page, then write underneath each feeling about why you feel that way.**

SHOCKED
Don't expect something to happen

HAPPY
Glad because something good happened

SAD
Unhappy or upset

ANGRY
Upset when you don't like what happened

SCARED
Afraid when something bad happens

CONFUSED
Don't know what something means

GUILTY
Feeling bad for something you think you did wrong

PROUD
Feeling good about something you did well

LONELY
Feeling all alone

NERVOUS
Thinking something bad is going to happen

RELIEVED
No longer worried about something

JEALOUS
Upset when you don't have something someone else has

DISAPPOINTED
Upset when things don't go the way you want

LOVED
Feeling cared for

(Add any other feelings you have about the divorce)

36

My Feelings about My Parents' Divorce

**Glue Feeling
Face Here**

I feel this way about
the divorce because:

_____
_____
_____

**Glue Feeling
Face Here**

I feel this way about
the divorce because:

_____
_____
_____

**Glue Feeling
Face Here**

I feel this way about
the divorce because:

_____
_____
_____

**Glue Feeling
Face Here**

I feel this way about
the divorce because:

_____
_____
_____

**Glue Feeling
Face Here**

I feel this way about
the divorce because:

_____
_____
_____

**Glue Feeling
Face Here**

I feel this way about
the divorce because:

_____
_____
_____

**Glue Feeling
Face Here**

I feel this way about
the divorce because:

_____
_____
_____

**Glue Feeling
Face Here**

I feel this way about
the divorce because:

_____
_____
_____

**Glue Feeling
Face Here**

I feel this way about
the divorce because:

_____
_____
_____

**Glue Feeling
Face Here**

I feel this way about
the divorce because:

_____
_____
_____

**Glue Feeling
Face Here**

I feel this way about
the divorce because:

_____
_____
_____

**Glue Feeling
Face Here**

I feel this way about
the divorce because:

_____
_____
_____

The Feelings Tic-Tac-Toe Game
(Supplies: Two different kinds of small wrapped candy, 4 of each kind)

It can be hard to talk about feelings, but sometimes playing a game can make it easier. To play this special version of *Tic-Tac-Toe*, use candy instead of X's and O's. Players take turns placing their candy on one of the nine squares on the game board in an attempt to get either an uninterrupted horizontal, vertical, or diagonal line of three. As the candy pieces are placed on a particular feeling on the game board, players describe a time they experienced that particular feeling. Players can eat one candy each time they win a round.

Happy	**Angry**	**Nervous**
Scared	**Loved**	**Guilty**
Jealous	**Sad**	**Relieved**

Something for Your Feel Better Bag:
Feelings Tic-Tac-Toe

(Supplies: Two different kinds of small wrapped candy, 4 of each kind)

Add the *Feelings Tic-Tac-Toe* sheet to your *Feel Better Bag*, along with some candy. Play the game with an adult helper. Playing the game with the adults who care about you is a good way to express yourself and let them know how you are feeling.

Happy	**Angry**	**Nervous**
Scared	**Loved**	**Guilty**
Jealous	**Sad**	**Relieved**

My Parents' Divorce: The Dice Game
(Supplies: Dice, bag filled with small prizes)

The Dice Game **will help you share your thoughts and feelings about your parents' divorce. To play the game, roll the dice. If you roll an even number (2, 4, 6), answer a question below in order from 1 to 6. If you roll an odd number (1, 3, 5), you get a small prize! Play the game until all the questions below have been answered.**

(1) When and how did you find out your parents were getting divorced? (Who told you? What did they say? What were you thinking and feeling when you found out?)

(2) Why do you think your parents divorced?

(3) What's something you worried about when your parents divorced?

(4) What's been the hardest part about your parents' divorce?

(5) Write about two changes that have happened in your life since the divorce (they could be changes you liked or changes you didn't like):

(6) What's something your parents can do to make it easier for you?

Something for Your Feel Better Bag:
Four Breathing
(Supplies: 4 stickers)

Taking slow deep breaths is a good way to help your body relax and feel better. Here is an easy way to learn how to take slow deep breaths; it's called *The Four Breathing* technique:

Think of the number **4**. As you are thinking about the number **4**, follow these **4** steps:

Step 1: Breathe in for **4** seconds

Step 2: Breathe out for **4** seconds

Step 3: Wait **4** seconds

Step 4: Repeat this **4** times

Put these instructions in your *Feel Better Bag* as a reminder to practice *Four Breathing*. Practice *Four Breathing* 4 times this week at bedtime, and get a sticker each time you practice this technique. If you practice *Four Breathing*, you will learn it so you can use it when you need to help your body relax.

How I Think, Feel, and Behave
(Supplies: ¼" adhesive dots, available in label section of office supply stores)

Below are some common ways children think, feel, and behave when their parents divorce. Read each statement and stick a dot beside the ones that apply to you. You can put more dots beside the ones you experience a lot.

1. I HAVE MORE WORRIES SINCE MY PARENTS DIVORCED _____

2. I HAVE BAD DREAMS _____

3. I HAVE SCARY THOUGHTS ABOUT BAD THINGS THAT HAPPENED TO ME _____

4. I SOMETIMES GET STOMACHACHES WHEN I FEEL UPSET _____

5. I'M WORRIED ABOUT SOMEONE IN MY FAMILY _____

6. I THINK I WILL HAVE AN UNHAPPY LIFE _____

7. SOMETIMES I WISH I WAS DEAD _____

8. I THINK THE DIVORCE WAS MY FAULT _____

9. I WISH MY PARENTS WOULD GET BACK TOGETHER _____

10. MY PARENTS ARGUE A LOT _____

11. MY PARENTS TELL ME MEAN THINGS ABOUT EACH OTHER _____

12. MY PARENT DOESN'T WANT ME TO SEE MY OTHER PARENT _____

13. MY MOM/DAD ARE FIGHTING ABOUT WHICH PARENT I SHOULD LIVE WITH _____

14. I FEEL I HAVE TO TAKE SIDES AND LOVE ONE PARENT MORE _____

15. IT'S HARD GOING BACK AND FORTH BETWEEN TWO HOMES _____

16. I FEEL VERY ANGRY ABOUT THE DIVORCE _____

17. I GET INTO TROUBLE A LOT _____

18. I THINK I'M IN THERAPY BECAUSE I AM BAD _____

19. I'M WORRIED I'M NOT DOING WELL IN SCHOOL _____

20. I GET TEASED BY OTHER KIDS _____

21. SOMEONE IS HURTING ME BUT I'M AFRAID TO TELL _____

22. I'M GLAD I'M GETTING HELP NOW _____

Something for Your Feel Better Bag:
The Spaghetti Technique
(Supplies: Uncooked spaghetti noodle in a Ziploc bag)

You can help your body feel better by learning to relax your muscles. Here's an easy way to learn how to relax your muscles; it's called *The Spaghetti Technique*:

Step 1: Stand up straight and stiff, tighten your body like uncooked spaghetti, hold it for 3 seconds

Step 2: Go limp and wiggle your muscles like cooked spaghetti

Step 3: Make your body go like wet spaghetti until you feel relaxed

Add these instructions and a spaghetti noodle to your *Feel Better Bag*. Practice *The Spaghetti Technique* every night this week before you go to sleep. It will help your body relax and feel better!

Butterflies in My Stomach

Everyone has problems and worries. This activity will help you talk about your problems and worries. It is called *Butterflies in My Stomach* because when you are worried or nervous about something, your stomach might feel funny or jittery, as if you have butterflies in your stomach. You don't *really* have butterflies in your stomach, it just feels like you do. Write your worries on the paper butterflies on the next page. Write bigger worries on the larger butterflies, smaller worries on the smaller ones. After you write your worries on the butterflies, answer the questions below:

When you are feeling scared or worried, what could you do to help yourself feel better?

Who are some people who can help you with your problems and worries? What can they do to help?

Butterfly Outlines

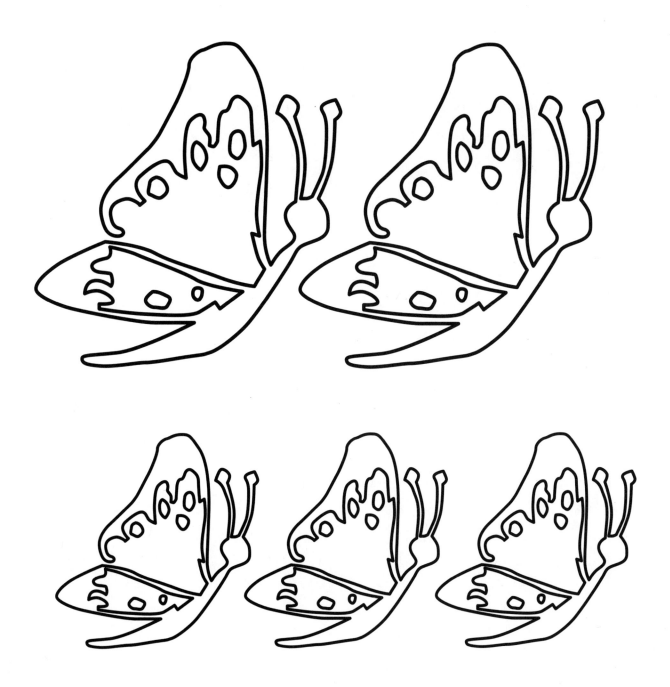

Something for Your Feel Better Bag:
Drink Something Warm and Soothing
(Supplies: Packet of hot chocolate, hot water, cup)

Drinking something warm is very soothing and can help you relax when you are upset. Ask a grown-up at home to help you make a cup of hot chocolate. While you are drinking it, think about how calm and relaxed it makes you feel.

People in My World
(Supplies: Heart and star stickers, Band-Aids, red and blue ¼" adhesive dots, available in office supply stores)

This activity will help you talk about the important people in your world. The first step is to fill in the picture of the world on the next page by writing the names of the people in your world. (Write each name in a different section on the world.) Include people who are important because you feel close with them, as well as people who are important because they have hurt or upset you. Be sure to include yourself, your mother, father, brothers, sisters, other people you live with, and other important people in your family. You may wish to include some of your relatives, teacher, therapist, best friend, pet, etc. Next, use stickers and symbols for the following feelings:

Put <u>hearts</u> on people in your world who <u>love</u> you. How do they show that they love you?

Put <u>Band-Aids</u> on people in your world who feel <u>sad</u>. Why do they feel sad?

Put <u>red dot stickers</u> on people in your world who feel <u>angry</u>. Why do they feel angry?

Put <u>blue dot stickers</u> on people in your world who feel <u>scared</u>. Why do they feel scared?

Put an <u>"X"</u> on people in your world who are <u>mean or bad</u>. Why are they mean or bad?

Put <u>star stickers</u> on people in your world who <u>help</u> you. What do they do to help you?

People in My World

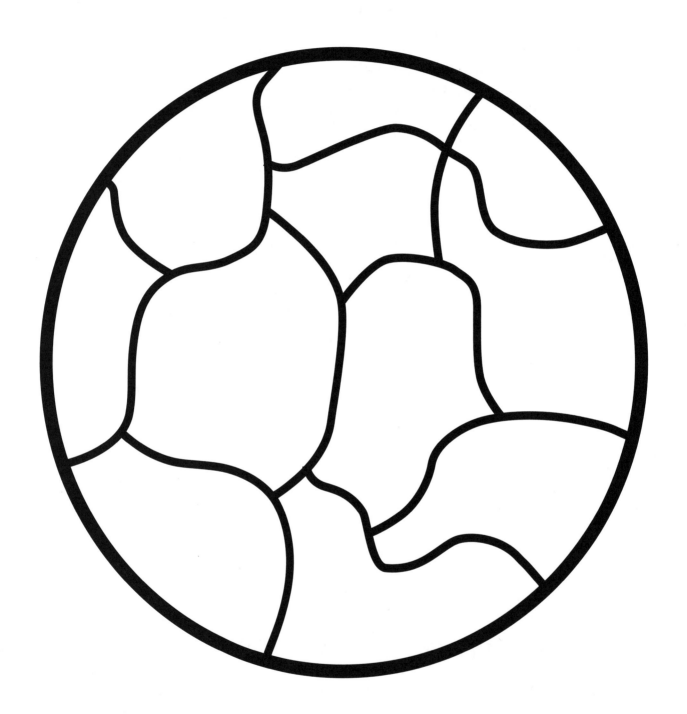

Something for Your Feel Better Bag: My Helpers
(Supplies: Bear sticker)

Put a bear sticker in your *Feel Better Bag* as a reminder that there are people in your world to help you. When you are upset, talk to one of your helpers.

Life's Ups & Downs
(Supplies: Paper, tape, ruler, 3"x 2" self-adhesive labels)

Life is full of ups and downs. We all experience both happy and sad times. Make a time-line of important events in your life, including both the good and bad times. To make a time-line, tape paper together to make one long piece. Use a ruler to draw a line across the middle of the paper. Think about important memories (happy and sad ones) and write each one on a separate adhesive label. Write your age at the time of the memory at the top of each label. Once you have written your memories on the labels, stick them on the time-line, beginning with your earliest memory and proceeding in order to more recent memories. Stick your <u>happy</u> memories <u>above</u> the line, and your <u>sad</u> memories <u>below</u> the line. If you are having trouble remembering things, use the following as a guide:

Earliest memory from when I was very young

Happy or sad memories with my family

Happy or sad memories of school

Memories of times I felt excited, scared, mad, guilty, loved

Memories of births, deaths, holidays, vacations, moves

Memories of when I or someone in my family got hurt or very sick

Memories of my achievements or proud moments

Worst day of my life

Best day of my life

Something for Your Feel Better Bag:
Tummy Breathing
(Supplies: Small toy)

Helping your body learn to relax is a good way to help yourself feel better. One way to help your body relax is to do *Tummy Breathing*. Lie on the floor, and place a small toy on your tummy. Breathe deeply in and out. Make the toy on your tummy rise during inhaling. Slowly count backward from 5 while breathing in through the nose, and then slowly breathe out through your mouth while again counting backward from 5. As you are slowly breathing in and out, make sure the toy on your tummy rises up each time you breathe in and goes down each time you breathe out. Put the toy in your *Feel Better Bag* as a reminder to practice *Tummy Breathing*. If you practice *Tummy Breathing* at least four times every night before you go to bed, you will learn it so you can use it when you need to help your body relax.

Spending Time with My Mother and Father

Because your parents are separated or divorced, you are sometimes with your mother, and sometimes with your father. Draw a picture of you and your mother doing something together, and you and your father doing something together, then answer the questions below:

Picture of me and Mom doing something together:

What I like about time spent with Mom:

What I don't like about time spent with Mom:

Picture of me and Dad doing something together:

What I like about time spent with Dad:

What I don't like about time spent with Dad:

Something for Your Feel Better Bag: Photo of my Parents

Ask your parents for a photograph of themselves for your *Feel Better Bag*. Ask them to write a little note to you on the back of the photo. Next time you are feeling upset, look at the photos and the notes as a reminder of how much your parents love you.

Section 5

Interventions to Address Divorce Issues

The interventions in this section help children actively understand, explore, and express feelings about divorce. Activities are included to help children work through a variety of divorce-specific issues, such as transitioning between two homes, dealing with parental conflict, working through loss, anger, and self-blame, and resolving reunification fantasies. A variety of play-based techniques are used, as they are less threatening and promote communication and mastery of the emotions and challenges brought about by divorce. The selection and pacing of interventions in this section should be based on the specific treatment needs of the child, as well as the child's readiness to confront his or her issues.

Interventions

Marriage and Divorce/Divorce: How It Works: Although parents may have explained the divorce to their children, children benefit from an appropriate explanation from a neutral person. These activities explain divorce and related issues, and help children begin to express their feelings regarding the divorce. If using *Divorce: How It Works* and *Question Box* in group therapy, group members can take turns picking a question from the box and reading it aloud to the rest of the group. Group members can be encouraged to add their own questions to the question box.

My Parents Love Me Forever: Children often feel that they are being rejected or that they are unlovable when parents divorce. It is important to reinforce the message that even when parents stop loving each other, they continue to love their children. If using this activity in a family session (child with one parent), the parent can reinforce his or her love for the child by writing a loving message inside the heart, and the child and parent can decorate the heart together.

Changes in My Life: This activity explores changes and disruptions in the child's daily life since the divorce, as well as the child's coping style. It also helps children examine positive changes that may occur after divorce.

Going Back and Forth Between Homes Air Hockey Game/Luggage Tag: Transitioning between two homes can be difficult for children. They must adapt to changing schedules and physical spaces, and decide what items should be with them in each home. The *Going Back and Forth Between Homes Air Hockey Game* uses an engaging and active game to help make the transition easier. The *Luggage Tag* activity also helps to ease the transition of going back and forth between homes. In addition, it facilitates communication between parents so they do not use the child as a messenger.

My Parents Argue and I Feel Stuck in the Middle/The Caught In the Middle Scribble Game/My Parents Are Fighting Over Me: Children who witness ongoing conflict between their parents or who feel pressured to choose sides are at risk for greater emotional difficulties. These interventions help children work through feelings associated with parental conflict and loyalty binds. They help children to disengage from marital conflict, which is an important psychological task for children of divorce. Once children are able to disengage from the marital conflict, they can better focus on their own lives and proceed with age-appropriate activities. In processing these interventions, it is important not to tarnish the parents, even if children voice negative feelings toward their parents. The practitioner can highlight that everyone makes mistakes, even parents, and when parents are angry at each other, they may say or do things that they shouldn't. If parents are in counseling, it can be conveyed that they are working hard to make things better.

I Am Angry at My Parent/Billy's Story: Some children become alienated from a parent after separation or divorce. They develop polarized, distorted perceptions toward their parents, in which they view one parent as all good and the other as all bad. A significant treatment goal for these children is to help transform their views of one parent as all good and the other as all bad into more balanced, realistic views. These two interventions are for use with alienated children. The goal of *I Am Angry at My Parent* is to help the child express feelings toward the rejected parent, and explore the changes that both the child and the parent need to make in order to foster a more positive relationship. *Billy's Story* aims to help the alienated child gain insight into his or her feelings and behaviors, challenge his or her distorted, polarized thinking, and ready the child to embrace a more positive relationship with the rejected parent. Treating alienated children is complex and must involve a comprehensive intervention plan that includes both the aligned and rejected parents. These activities will not be effective unless the aligned and rejected parents have made significant gains in therapy, i.e. the aligned parent can genuinely support the child's relationship with the other parent, and the rejected parent can appropriately respond to the child's emotional needs.

I Wish My Parents Would Get Back Together: It is common for children of divorce to fantasize about their parents reuniting. But an important psychological task is for children to accept the permanence of the divorce, so they do not remain stuck trying to get their parents back together. This activity facilitates this task.

Sometimes My Parent Misses Visits: Some parents consistently miss scheduled visits with their children. This usually leaves children feeling angry and disappointed. Children need an opportunity to express these feelings within the safety and neutrality of the therapeutic environment.

There Was Violence in My Family: If children witnessed domestic abuse in their families, this is a separate issue from the divorce that needs to be addressed. This intervention assesses the child's reaction to the abuse, such as sensory assault and intrusive thoughts. If the activity uncovers a trauma response, additional treatment interventions will be necessary. Since the activity may trigger flashbacks or anxiety, it can be helpful to teach or review a previously learned relaxation strategy prior to beginning the activity, so the child can use the strategy to self-soothe if needed. If the child is having access with a parent who was abusive, the child may be fearful of this parent, even if the abuse has stopped. These feelings must be addressed and appropriate safeguards put in place to ensure the child's safety.

I Don't See My Parent Anymore: Children may be estranged from a parent either because their parent abandoned the family, or because access with a parent was terminated. Loss of contact with a parent can leave children feeling confused, sad, angry, guilty, or rejected. This activity explores the child's feelings and possible misconceptions related to the estrangement. It normalizes the child's feelings and helps to diffuse feelings of guilt. It also emphasizes the love and care the other parent has for the child, which is an important reassuring message. If the child has not been given a truthful and age-appropriate explanation for the estrangement, this should be done by the therapist, preferably together with the child's parent. An appropriate explanation will help the child understand that the absent parent has problems and that there is nothing wrong with the child. For children who have been abandoned by a parent, it is helpful to establish a relationship between the child and a same-sex substitute for the absent parent, such as a relative or volunteer from the organization Big Brothers/Big Sisters. A long-term relationship with a caring parent substitute will help the child feel loved and valued.

My Parents Are Dating/My Parents Are Getting Remarried: Most divorced parents eventually begin dating and many remarry. Some children want their parents to remarry, as they wish their parent to be happier and less lonely or they want to live in a two-parent family again. However, many children feel angry, jealous, or displaced when their parents find other mates. Sessions with the child, parent, and new partner may be helpful in resolving problematic issues. Individual sessions with children can focus on helping them to express their feelings, assert their need for more time and attention from their parents, and be reassured of their parents' lasting love for them.

Basketball: A Game About Divorce: This game helps children integrate the concepts that were covered in the preceding activities on divorce. Modifying the traditional game of basketball can engage children. Blank cards can be added so clients can make up their own questions for the game.

Marriage and Divorce
(Supplies: Scissors, transparent tape)

It can be hard talking about divorce, so let's do a puzzle to make it easier. Prepare the puzzle by cutting along the dotted lines below. Then complete one puzzle piece at a time, in order from one to five. Once you have completed all five puzzle pieces, put the puzzle together, tape it on both sides, and put it in this book.

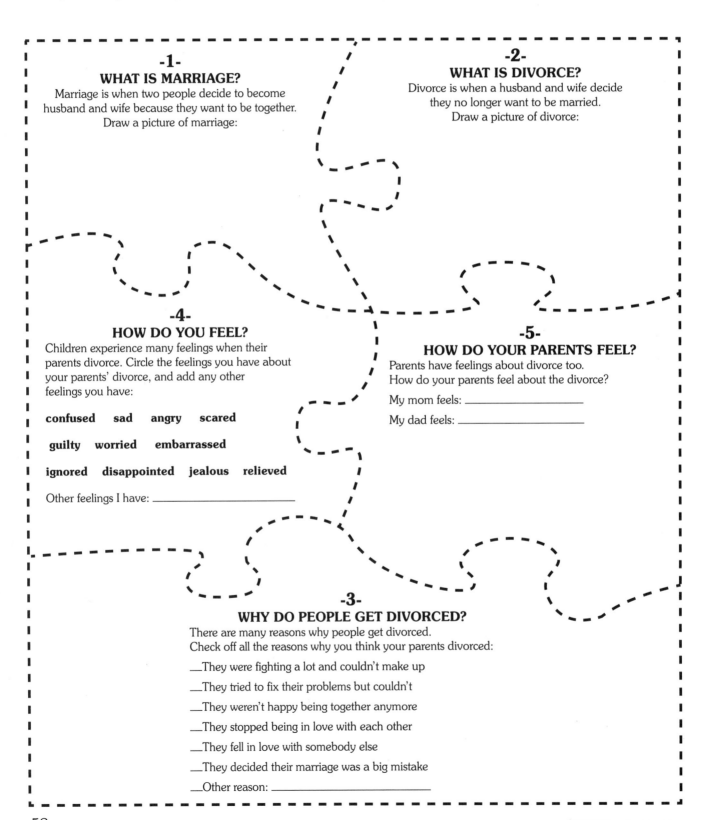

-1-
WHAT IS MARRIAGE?
Marriage is when two people decide to become husband and wife because they want to be together.
Draw a picture of marriage:

-2-
WHAT IS DIVORCE?
Divorce is when a husband and wife decide they no longer want to be married.
Draw a picture of divorce:

-4-
HOW DO YOU FEEL?
Children experience many feelings when their parents divorce. Circle the feelings you have about your parents' divorce, and add any other feelings you have:

confused   sad   angry   scared

guilty   worried   embarrassed

ignored   disappointed   jealous   relieved

Other feelings I have: _____

-5-
HOW DO YOUR PARENTS FEEL?
Parents have feelings about divorce too.
How do your parents feel about the divorce?

My mom feels: _____

My dad feels: _____

-3-
WHY DO PEOPLE GET DIVORCED?
There are many reasons why people get divorced.
Check off all the reasons why you think your parents divorced:

___They were fighting a lot and couldn't make up

___They tried to fix their problems but couldn't

___They weren't happy being together anymore

___They stopped being in love with each other

___They fell in love with somebody else

___They decided their marriage was a big mistake

___Other reason: _____

Something for Your Feel Better Bag:
Bubble Bath
(Supplies: Bubble Bath)

Taking a bubble bath is a good way to help your body feel calm and relaxed. Add the bubble bath to your *Feel Better Bag* and use it when you need to.

Divorce: How It Works
(Note to therapist: See next page for activity preparation)

You may have a lot of questions and mixed up feelings about your parents' divorce. So here is a quick explanation about how divorce works:

First of all, it is important for you to know that divorce doesn't happen right away. First parents separate. <u>Separation</u> is when parents stop being together. Usually one parent moves out of the house and finds another place to live. Sometimes after living apart for a while, parents decide to get back together. But usually they decide to get a <u>divorce</u>, which means they want to stop being married forever.

Once parents decide to divorce, there are many important decisions that have to be made, like who will live where (<u>custody</u>), and how much time the children will spend with each parent (<u>visitation</u>). Sometimes parents disagree about these big decisions and have a <u>custody battle</u>. You may notice your parents arguing or even being mean to each other during this time. But it is important for you to know that no matter what happens, your parents love you very much.

Parents may get lawyers. A <u>lawyer</u> is an adult who helps parents understand the laws and rules about divorce. Each parent may have his or her own lawyer. Sometimes parents go to a mediator. A <u>mediator</u> is someone who listens to both parents and helps them figure things out and decide what is fair. If they still can't decide, then they go to a special building called <u>court</u> where the judge works, and they tell the judge what they want. The <u>judge</u> is someone who makes the final decisions for the family, like where the children should live, and how much time they should spend with each of their parents. The judge decides what is best for everybody.

It can take a long time, sometimes years, for parents to get a divorce. This is because big decisions have to be made when parents divorce, so it takes time for all the adults (parents, lawyers, mediators, judges) to work out what is best. The most important thing for you to know is that when parents divorce each other, they don't divorce their kids. Divorced parents still love their children very much!

You may still have questions about divorce. The *Question Box* will help to answer some of your questions. Take turns with your therapist picking a card from the *Question Box* and reading it out loud. If you pick a blank card, write your own question on it and see if you and your therapist can answer it. To make this activity more fun, there are some special surprise cards in the box!

Question Box
(Supplies: Box, scissors, bag filled with prizes)

(Note to therapist: To prepare the *Question Box*, cut out the cards below, fold them, and place them in a box labeled *Question Box*.)

Question: How long does it take for children to stop feeling sad about their parents' divorce? **Answer**: Not as long as you think. But talking about feelings is a good way to get the sadness out and begin to feel better.	**Question**: Is it okay for children to play and have fun even while their parents are unhappy about the divorce? **Answer**: Yes! Children can still be happy and have fun while their parents are solving their problems. Besides, it may help parents feel better if they see that their children are happy.
Question: If one parent has left, will the other parent leave the children too? **Answer**: No! When one parent leaves, the other will take care of the children.	**Question**: Is it up to children to decide which parent to live with? **Answer**: No! Deciding where children should live is too big a decision for children to make. Parents will sort this out or they will get help from a lawyer, mediator, or judge.
Question: What is custody? **Answer:** Custody is a legal word for the parent in charge of taking care of the children and making big decisions like where the children will live and go to school. Joint custody is when both parents agree that they will share in all the responsibilities and decisions about the children.	**Question:** If parents stop loving each other, will they stop loving their children too? **Answer:** No! Even when parents divorce and stop loving each other, they still love their children no matter what!
Make up your own question about divorce	**Make up your own question about divorce**
Make up your own question about divorce	**Make up your own question about divorce**
Pick something from the Prize Bag!	**Pick something from the Prize Bag!**

Something for Your Feel Better Bag: Divorce Dictionary

Make your own *Mini Divorce Dictionary* to put in your *Feel Better Bag*. Cut out the squares below, stack them, and staple them together on the left side to make a book. Next time you hear a word that you don't understand, you can look it up in your *Divorce Dictionary*.

My Mini
Divorce Dictionary

My Name:

_____

Separation:
When parents stop being together

Divorce:
When parents decide to stop being husband and wife. A divorce is a legal end to a marriage.

Lawyer:
An adult who helps parents understand the laws and rules about divorce. Each parent may have his or her own lawyer. Sometimes the lawyer helps parents tell the judge their side of the story. Sometimes children have their own lawyer or a person called an advocate who tells the judge what they feel about the divorce.

Mediator:
Someone who listens to both parents and helps them figure things out about the divorce and decide what's fair.

Judge:
Someone who makes the rules for the divorce, like where the children should live, and when they should have visits with their parents.

Court:
The building where parents go to get a divorce.

Visitation:
A schedule of when children will see or stay with each of their parents.

Custody:
A legal word for the parent who is in charge of taking care of the children and making the big decisions like where the children will live and go to school.

My Parents Love Me Forever

Your parents may have divorced because they stopped loving each o
Sometimes love between parents can end. But love between parents and th
children is the kind of love that never ends. It is forever love. So even if you
parents stopped loving each other, they still love you forever! Cut out the heart
below and decorate it. Add it to your *Feel Better Bag* as a reminder that your
parents love you forever.

My Parents Love Me Forever

Changes in My Life

...anges that happen when parents split up. Change means
...ent. When parents split up, your life changes because
...ne, and things are different in how you feel. Some change
...nge feels sad or scary. Read the changes on the next page
...have had since your parents split up. If it's a change you
...de of this page under the happy face. If it's a change you
...right side of this page under the sad face.

Changes I Like 😊	Changes I Don't Like 🙁

**Talk with your therapist about the changes in your life, especially if the change
makes you feel sad, angry, or scared.**

**It can be hard to cope with change, but with time, you will begin to feel more
comfortable with the changes in your life.**

Changes in My Life Since My Parents Divorced

One of my parents moved out

We don't spend time together as a whole family

I moved to another house or apartment after the divorce

I live in two different places

I go back and forth between two homes

We have less money

I am left alone or with a babysitter more since the divorce

I don't see one of my parents very much

I don't see one of my parents anymore

My parent is dating or marrying someone else

My parents argue more

My parents argue less

I get to celebrate birthdays and holidays twice (one time with each parent)

I have new rules to follow

I get to spend less time with my friends

I feel a lot more upset

I get more attention

I get less attention

I get into more trouble

I act more grown up

Sometimes I act like a baby

I feel different from other kids

I have more chores to do

I have less fun with my family

I have more fun with my family

I am doing worse in school

Other changes: _____

Something for Your Feel Better Bag: Things that Stay the Same

When your parents split up, there are a lot of things that change. This can be upsetting. You can help yourself feel better by thinking about the things that are staying the same. Make a list of the things that are staying the same for you since your parents split up. Below are some examples to help you get started. Add the list to your *Feel Better Bag.* **Next time you feel upset about any changes in your life since your parents split up, look at the list of the things that are staying the same in your life.**

Things that are staying the same for me since my parents split up:

1. I still have the same color eyes

2. I still like to play

3. I still have _____

4. I still get to _____

5. I still like to _____

6. I still have a parent who _____

Going Back & Forth Between Homes Air Hockey Game
(Supplies: Two straws, masking tape, paper)

It can be hard to go back and forth between your mother's home and your father's home. The *Going Back and Forth Between Two Homes Air Hockey Game* will help you talk about this. To make the hockey rink, follow the instructions on the next page. The object of the game is for you and your therapist to work together to blow the hockey puck as fast as you can back and forth from one end (*MOM'S HOME*) to the other end (*DAD'S HOME*). To begin the game, you should both kneel down on the floor beside the hockey rink. Place the puck in the center of the rink. Put the straws in your mouth, and place the other end of the straws just behind the hockey puck. At the count of three, together blow into the straws and blow the hockey puck toward the space marked *MOM'S HOME*. Once you have blown the puck into mom's net, blow it toward the other end, into the space marked *DAD'S HOME*. (If the hockey puck gets blown outside the hockey rink, place it back in the middle of the rink and begin again.) Once you have successfully blown the puck from one end to the other, choose a *Help Card* and read it aloud. The *Help Cards* are tips to make it easier to go back and forth between your two homes. You can take the cards home and add them to your *Feel Better Bag*. Play several rounds of *Air Hockey*, and take a new *Help Card* after each time you blow the puck from one end of the rink to the other. For added fun, you can time yourselves and see if you can beat your record and move the puck faster from one end to the other. At the end of the game, answer the questions below:

Is it easy or hard for you to go back and forth between homes? What makes it easy? What makes it hard?

Who decided on the schedule of when you are at your mom's, and when you are at your dad's? How do you feel about this schedule?

Are there times when you don't want to go to your other parent's home? How come?

Are there different rules and routines at your two homes? Please explain:

Air Hockey Rink

Use tape to make the rink. Begin by clearing a large space on the floor. To make the hockey rink, tape two pieces of masking tape along the floor (each piece of tape should be about 4 feet long, and placed about 1-2 feet apart.) Use tape to make the nets by placing tape at each end of the rink in the shape of a U. Place a piece of masking tape inside one net and write *MOM'S HOME* on it. Place a piece of tape inside the other net and write *DAD'S HOME* on it. To make the puck, crumple a piece of three-inch square paper into a wad. Place the puck in the center of the rink. (Use the diagram below as a guide. The dotted lines are the tape.)

Help Cards

Below are some tips to make it easier to go back and forth between two homes. Cut out the cards and place them face up on the table.

Put a calendar in your room. Write *Mom* on days you are with your mom, and write *Dad* on days when you are with your dad. This will help you keep track.

Create a private space at each home for your clothes, toys, books, and other belongings. Ask your parents to help by saying, "This is my home with you. Can we find a private space just for my stuff?"

Keep certain things at each home so you don't have to pack as much, like a toothbrush, pajamas, and some clothes.

Have a favorite toy, book, or game at each home so you always have something fun to do.

Keep something comforting at each home, like a stuffed animal, or a special blanket, so you feel safe and comforted no matter where you are.

Follow the same routine at each home so it's easier to adjust. For example, get up and go to bed at the same time at each home.

Make a special area to do homework, like a desk or table that you always use.

When you are at your mother's, keep a picture of your father with you. When you are at your father's, keep a picture of your mother with you. This will help you feel close to both your parents when you are apart from them.

Luggage Tag

(Supplies: Luggage tag with clear plastic cover, wallet size photo of each parent,
cardboard, scissors, Post-It Notes)

**When your parents are divorced, you have to travel back and forth between two
different homes. It may be hard to remember which days you are with your mom,
and which days you are with your dad and it may be hard to remember what to
bring with you. The *Luggage Tag* activity will help you remember when you are
with each parent, and what to bring with you.**

Step 1: Make a Luggage Tag

Place a wallet size photo of each of your parents in a luggage tag. (Use a ready-made luggage
tag or make your own out of cardboard, Ziploc bag, and durable string. If you cannot get a
wallet size photo of each parent, you can draw a picture of each of them instead.)

Step 2: Make a Packing List

Cut out a piece of cardboard (about 2"x 2" or small enough to slide easily into the luggage
tag). Write at the top of this cardboard: "Packing List" and, below it, write what you need to
pack in your bag whenever you go to your mom's or your dad's home. For example, your
favorite stuffed animal, toothbrush, change of clothes, homework, or anything else you need
to have with you. (It may help to ask your parents to add to this list.) Slip this list into your
luggage tag.

Step 3: Cut Out the Letters to Your Parents

Cut out the letters to your mom and dad on the next page, and give the letters to your parents.
Give your parents the Post-It Notes.

Step 4: Take the Luggage Tag Home and Attach it to Your Bag

Take your Luggage Tag home and attach it to the bag you pack when you travel to your
mom's or your dad's home. When you are going to be with your mom, place the photo of
your mom on top in your Luggage Tag. (Place the photo of your dad underneath the photo
of your mom in your Luggage Tag.) This will remind you that you are with your mom on that
day or weekend. When you are going to be with your dad, place the photo of your dad on
top in your Luggage Tag. (Place the photo of your mom underneath the photo of your dad in
your luggage tag.) This will remind you that you are with your dad on that day or weekend.
Look at your packing list to make sure you have packed everything you need. Check to see if
your parent has put a Post-It Note on your Luggage Tag with any important reminders.

Step 5: Look at the Photo of Your Parent if You Need To

If you are at your mom's and you miss your dad, look at the photo of your dad. This will help
you feel close to him. If you are at your dad's and you miss your mom, look at the photo of
your mom. This will help you feel close to her.

Letters to Mom and Dad

Have your parents join the session, and read the following note to them. (If you don't want to read the note, you can ask your therapist to read it for you.)

Dear Mom,

Traveling back and forth between two homes is tough on kids. It can be hard to remember when I'm supposed to go to Dad's and what I have to bring with me when I go there. My luggage tag will help me to remember. I will put the photo of Dad in the luggage tag on the day I am supposed to go there and I will look at my packing list to help me remember what to bring with me. Please put a Post-It Note on my luggage tag with any important reminders, for example, "Take the school bus home to Dad's today" or "Take your soccer uniform for your soccer practice at 4:00 today."
Thanks for helping to make it easier when I go to Dad's.

Love,

_____

Dear Dad,

Traveling back and forth between two homes is tough on kids. It can be hard to remember when I'm supposed to go to Mom's and what I have to bring with me when I go there. My luggage tag will help me to remember. I will put the photo of Mom in the luggage tag on the day I am supposed to go there and I will look at my packing list to help me remember what to bring with me. Please put a Post-It Note on my luggage tag with any important reminders, for example, "Take the school bus home to Mom's today" or "Take your soccer uniform for your soccer practice at 4:00 today."
Thanks for helping to make it easier when I go to Mom's.

Love,

_____

My Parents Argue and I Feel Stuck in the Middle
(Supplies: Marshmallows, pretzel sticks, icing)

Your parents may be angry with each other, and they may argue. They may yell at each other or say mean words. This may make you feel sad, scared, or angry. Answer the questions below:

My parents argue about _____

_____

When they argue, they _____

When my parents argue, I feel _____

My mom says mean things to my dad, like _____

_____

My dad says mean things to my mom, like _____

_____

Marshmallow People

Make 3 marshmallow people to represent you, your mother, and your father (use marshmallows for the head and body, pretzel sticks for the arms and legs, and icing for the face and hair). Use the marshmallow people to act out an argument you saw between your parents. Then have the marshmallow person that represents you say the following statement out loud to your mother and father marshmallow people: "It upsets me when you argue in front of me. Please stop."

If your parents don't stop arguing in front of you, go to another room, so you cannot hear them arguing. Use the marshmallow person that represents you to practice going into another room so you cannot hear your parents arguing.

When your parents are arguing, it can help to tell yourself: "When my parents argue, they still love me, no matter what!" Use your marshmallow person to practice saying this to yourself.

(You can eat the marshmallow people at the end of this activity!)

Note to Parents

Have your parents join the session, and read the following note to them. (If you don't want to read the note, you can ask your therapist to read it for you).

Dear Mom and Dad,

It upsets me when you argue in front of me, or tell me mean things about each other. I have learned that it is okay to politely ask you to stop. So next time you argue in front of me, or tell me mean things about each other, I am going to politely say, "Please stop." If you continue to argue, I will go to another room so I cannot hear you arguing. Thank you for doing your best,

Love,

_____

Something for Your Feel Better Bag: What I Can Do When My Parents Argue

When your parents argue in front of you, you can help yourself by following the three steps below. Cut this out and add it to your *Feel Better Bag.*

This is what I can do when my parents argue in front of me:

1. Politely say: "It upsets me when you argue in front of me. Please stop."

2. Go into another room where you cannot hear them arguing.

3. Tell yourself: "Even though my parents argue, they still love me."

The Caught in the Middle Scribble Game
(Large sheet of durable paper or cardboard, two different colored water soluble markers)

Children often feel caught in the middle when their parents divorce. This is because their parents are fighting and they are in the middle of it. The *Caught in the Middle Scribble Game* will help you talk about these feelings. To play, sit on the floor opposite your therapist. Place the sheet of paper between you. Select a marker and give a different color marker to your therapist. On one end of the paper, write *MOM*, and on the other end, write *DAD*. In the middle of the paper, write *MIDDLE* in big letters. This game is played like tag, but instead of tagging people, players tag markers. The object of the game is for the person who is "It" to catch the other player's marker with his or her marker. "It" must scribble fast to catch the other player's marker, while the other player must scribble fast so his or her marker does not get tagged or caught by "It." Decide which player is going to be "It." Place the tips of your markers down on the paper. Once the round begins, players must scribble with their markers as fast as they can, and they cannot lift their markers off the paper until "It" catches the other player's marker with his or her marker. Once the player's marker is tagged or caught by "It," change roles and have the other player be "It." After the game, talk about how children of divorce feel caught in the middle. Then answer the questions below:

How come children of divorce often feel caught in the middle?

How does it feel for a child to be caught in the middle?

What ideas do you have about how children can cope better with these feelings?

Something for Your Feel Better Bag:
Scribble my Tension Away
(Supplies: Water soluble marker and paper)

Scribbling hard onto paper is a good way to release tension in your body. Add a marker and some paper to your *Feel Better Bag*. Next time you are feeling upset, use the marker to scribble hard onto the paper. (Take care to scribble onto the paper and not onto anything else!) When you are done, tear the paper into pieces and throw it in the garbage.

My Parents are Fighting Over Me
(Supplies: Plastic people figurines)

Your parents may be fighting over who you should live with. Your mother may think you should live with her, and your father may think you should live with him. As your parents are fighting about this and trying to sort out who you will live with, they may act mean toward each other. It's hard for children to be in the middle of this fighting. The *Big Fight* is a story to help you talk about your feelings. Have your therapist read the story while you act it out with plastic people figurines. Then answer the questions below:

Why did Donna and Mike get married?

Why did Donna and Mike get divorced?

How did the fighting between Donna and Mike make the children feel?

Are your parents arguing about who you should live with? How does this make you feel?

What did the children learn from their therapist about having to pick sides? How did this make the children feel?

The Big Fight

When Donna and Mike Smith decided to get married, they were very much in love. They thought they would be together forever. They were very happy together at first, and they had two wonderful children whom they both loved very, very much. But after a while, they started to argue a lot, and have problems they couldn't fix. They weren't happy being together anymore, so they made a very big and difficult decision: they decided to get a divorce.

The divorce was tough on everyone. The fighting didn't stop. In fact, Donna and Mike started to argue even more, especially about whom the children were going to live with. Donna felt the children should live with her, and Mike thought the children should live with him. They argued and said horrible, mean things about each other in front of the children. The children didn't know if these things their parents said about each other were true or not, but they did know that the fighting and meanness made them feel very bad. The children felt caught in the middle. They didn't want to have to choose sides because they loved both their parents.

The children went to see a therapist whose job it was to help children with their problems and worries. The therapist helped them talk about their feelings. The therapist helped them understand that they didn't have to pick sides; they could love both their parents. The therapist told them that a judge would help their parents come up with a plan that was fair so the children could spend time with both their mom and their dad. The children felt so much better!

Something for Your Feel Better Bag: My Parents Love Me

If your parents are fighting over you, it is not because they want to hurt you, it is because they both love you so much! Make a list of the things your parents do to show that they love you. Add your list to your *Feel Better Bag* and look at it every once in a while, as a reminder of how much you are loved!

Ways my parents show me they love me:

1. _____

2. _____

3. _____

I Wish My Parents Would Get Back Together

Lots of children in divorced families wish their parents would get back together. They imagine their whole family living happily in one place. Sometimes children try to get their parents to make up or love each other again. But as much as you want your parents to get back together, the truth is, your wish will probably never come true. Divorced parents usually don't remarry each other or live together again. Once you realize this, you may feel sad. Your feelings are normal. The story, *Willy's Wishes and the Wise Wizard*, will help you talk about these feelings. Read the story, then answer the questions below.

How did Willy feel after his parents separated?

What special power does Willy (and each and every person) have? How does this special power help Willy?

Make a list of things that you *do* have:

Willy's Wishes and the Wise Wizard

This is a story about a boy named Willy. His real name is Willliam but most people call him Willy. Willy was a typical kid; he liked to play computer games and ride his bike, and he preferred dessert to eating vegetables! Willy led a pretty normal, happy life until something bad happened… his parents separated. Then his whole life changed. He felt very sad and angry, but he did not want to talk about these feelings with anyone. Because of his sad, angry feelings, Willy sometimes did things he never used to, like wetting his bed. He often had a nervous feeling that would give him stomachaches. Nighttime was especially difficult because he had a hard time falling asleep, and he often had scary dreams. Willy stopped laughing and playing and having fun. He spent much of his time in his secret hiding spot, curled up in a little ball. He would lie there for hours and think about how much better things would be if his parents were still together.

One day, while in his secret hiding spot, he fell asleep and dreamed the most wonderful dream — that he had magical powers and could make wishes come true! So, he wished for a new shiny red bike, and for chocolate fudge cake for dessert every day, and for his parents to get back together and — poof! — his wishes came true! He felt so happy! But then something startled him, and he woke up and realized it was just a dream. No new shiny red bike. No chocolate fudge cake for dessert every day. And worst of all, his parents had not gotten back together. He felt so sad. He buried his head in his teddy bear and cried.

Willy lay there for a long time and, after awhile, he fell asleep again. This time, he dreamed that a wizard came to him — a very old, wise wizard, named Waldorf. He had a long white beard, and he wore a long purple cape with bright yellow shiny stars and a tall pointy hat to match. But he did not have a magic wand. "You can't be a real wizard," said Willy, "because you do not have a magic wand." "Oh, but you see, my boy, I do not need a magic wand, for I have discovered a special power that does not require any magic." "What kind of special power?" asked Willy. "Well," replied Waldorf the Wizard, "It is a special power that will bring you happiness. It is the power to think about all that you have." "Huh, what do you mean?" asked Willy. "Well, instead of thinking about what you *do not* have, just think about what you *do* have. And if you think about all that you have, this will bring you happiness." "I wish I had that special power," said Willy. "Ah, but you do have this special power," replied Waldorf. "In fact, each and every person has this special power. They just have to use it." "So you mean I have this special power?" asked Willy. "Yes! I'll show you what I mean. First, think about what you do not have." "Well," said Willy, "I do not have a new shiny red bike. And I do not get to eat chocolate fudge cake for dessert every day. And worst of all, I do not have a mother and a father who live together." "And how do you feel when you think about what you do not have?" "I feel bad," replied Willy in a sad tone. "Now, think about what you *do* have." "Well, let's see, I have a bike that I got two years ago and it has a cool yellow banana seat that the kids on my street think is pretty neat. And I get chocolate fudge cake sometimes, like when it's my birthday. And I have a mother and a father who love me." "How do you feel now, as you think about what you *do* have?" "I feel better!" replied Willy with a smile on his face. "You see! You have the power to think about what you *do* have, and if you choose to use this power, you will feel better!" Just then, something startled Willy, and he woke up from his dream. He ran to his room and got a pen and paper. He made a list of all that he had. And whenever he started to feel sad, he looked at his list, and this made him feel better. "Wow!" he thought, "I do have special power!"

Something for Your Feel Better Bag: Feeling Happy for All That I Have

Look at the list of things that you *do* have. Choose three things from this list and write them below. Next time you feel upset, look at this list. And remember Waldorf the Wizard's message… if you think about what you *do* have, you will feel happier!

Sometimes My Parent Misses Visits

There may be times when your parent misses scheduled visits. It can feel very disappointing to get all excited about seeing your parent, and then he or she does not show up. Draw a picture below to show how you feel when your parent misses a visit:

It can help to get your feelings out by writing a story. Write a story about a child whose parent misses visits. Make sure your story has a beginning, middle, and end. You can write the story on your own, or together with your therapist.

Something for Your Feel Better Bag:
I Can Make it Through Tough Times
(Supplies: Happy face sticker)

Add a happy face sticker to your *Feel Better Bag* as a reminder of what a great job you did getting your feelings out! Next time you are feeling upset, look at this sticker and remember that you have gotten yourself through tough times in the past, and you can make it through tough times now.

I Am Angry at My Parent

When parents divorce, children may feel angry at one of their parents. They may blame the divorce on this parent. They may not want to be with this parent. Draw a picture to show how you feel toward this parent:

What bothers or upsets you about this parent?

What kind of parent do most kids need or want?

What changes does your parent need to make to be the parent most kids need or want?

What changes do you need to make to have a closer relationship with this parent?

How would your life be better if you had a close relationship with both your parents?

Something for Your Feel Better Bag: Think Positive

Thinking positive thoughts is a good way to help yourself feel better. Below are some examples of positive thoughts:

Nobody is perfect

I can feel good for all that I have

I am lovable

_____

_____

_____

Add your own positive thoughts to the list. Put the positive thoughts in your *Feel Better Bag*, and look at them when you are upset.

Billy's Story

***Billy's Story* is about a boy whose parents got divorced. Read the story, then answer the questions below.**

How did Billy's parents feel toward him when he was born?

What special activities did Billy used to do with his family and with each of his parents when he was a little boy?

Why did Billy's parents get divorced?

Why did Billy blame himself for his parents' divorce?

How did Billy feel toward his mom and dad after the divorce?

How come, after the divorce, Billy forgot about the good times he had with his dad? What helped him to remember these good times?

What do you think can be learned from this story?

Billy's Story

This is a story about a boy named Billy. When he was born, his mother held him close to her heart, cried tears of joy, and said it was the happiest day of her life. His father was so happy too. He cradled his newborn son in his arms, stared into his eyes, and felt such a strong love for his little baby boy.

As Billy grew, his parents loved him and cared for him. They spent time together as a family and sometimes went on special outings, like to the zoo. Billy loved it when his dad gave him piggyback rides and helped him build forts, or when he and his mom made model airplanes together. These were such fun, happy times. Of course, things weren't perfect. His parents sometimes argued and said mean things to each other. And like all kids, Billy sometimes did things he wasn't supposed to do, like using his mom's lipstick to color a picture on the wall, or forgetting to wipe his shoes and tracking mud all through the house. When he misbehaved, his parents would usually send him to his room or take away his favorite toy for a few days. Sometimes they would yell at him.

As Billy got older, he noticed that his parents started to yell a lot more, especially at each other. Then one day, his parents told him they were getting a divorce. They said it was because they were not happy being together anymore, but Billy wondered if it was because he was bad. His dad moved out. His mom cried. Billy felt sad but he tried not to show it because he didn't want to make his mom more upset. His mom didn't want him to see his dad because she said he was a bad person. Billy refused to see his dad. When his dad called him on the phone, Billy told him he was evil for ruining his family.

Billy started to get into trouble at school. When his teacher asked him what was wrong, he told her his dad was evil and had ruined his family. Billy was sent to see a therapist. When the therapist asked Billy to tell his feelings about his mom and dad, he said his mom was good and his dad was bad. When the therapist asked him to tell one good memory and one bad memory about each of his parents, Billy said he only had good memories of his mom, and only bad memories of his dad. He told the therapist that he never did anything fun with his dad, and his dad used to yell at him all the time.

The next week, Billy met with the therapist again, but this time his dad was there. His dad brought picture albums that showed his mom and dad when they first got married. There were pictures of Billy when he was a little boy, laughing and playing. The pictures reminded Billy of happier times, like when he and his dad used to feed the animals at the petting zoo and build huge forts in the backyard. Billy realized there were good times with his dad, but he had forgotten because he was so mad at his dad for leaving.

The therapist helped Billy let out his angry feelings, and he started to have fun again with his dad. His mom also went to talk to a therapist about her sad feelings, and she began to feel better, which made Billy feel better too. Although Billy was still sad that his parents were divorced, he felt good knowing that he had a mom and a dad who both loved him so much!

Something for Your Feel Better Bag: A Happy Memory

Go through your family photo albums and select a picture that shows a happy time spent with your parents. Put the photo in your *Feel Better Bag* as a reminder of the happy memories you have. (Don't forget to ask permission from your parents to have this photo.) If you cannot get a photo, then draw a picture of a happy memory with your parents, and put the drawing in your *Feel Better Bag*.

There Was Violence in My Family
(Supplies: Assortment of plastic animals)

There may have been bad fights in your family before or after the divorce. Maybe you saw your parent hurting your other parent. Or your parent may have hurt you. The police may have come to your house. This happens in some families, and it is a scary thing for children to go through. Choose an animal for each member of your family, and use the animals to act out a skit to show what happened when there was violence in your family. Then answer the questions below:

What did you see, hear, and feel when your parent hurt you or your other parent?

When the fighting was happening, what were you doing, thinking, and feeling?

When the fighting was happening, what was the scariest part?

What did you want to do when the fighting was happening?

Think of something you could do that would make you feel better right now:

Reading a book about violence in families will help you understand your situation better. Your therapist will choose a book for you to read together.

If there is still violence in your family or if you or someone in your family is being hurt, it is really important that you tell your therapist what's happening so the hurting can stop.

Something for Your Feel Better Bag: Call the Hotline

If you or someone you know is being hurt, it is really important that you tell an adult what's happening, so the hurting can stop. If you do not feel comfortable talking to an adult at home or at school, and you cannot reach your therapist, you can call the Girls and Boys Hotline*. Add the phone number to your *Feel Better Bag* so you can call it if you have no other adult to talk to about your sad or scared feelings.

Phone number for the Boys and Girls Hotline:
1-800-448-3000

*If you live in Canada, you can call the Kids Help Phone at: 1-800-668-6868. If you live outside Canada or the United States, your therapist will give you a phone number you can call.

I Don't See My Parent Anymore

After the divorce, you may have stopped seeing one of your parents. Below are some common reactions children have in this situation. Read each statement and color in the circle to show how you feel. If you feel that way a lot, color in the whole circle. If you feel that way a bit, color in part of the circle. If you don't feel that way at all, leave the circle blank.

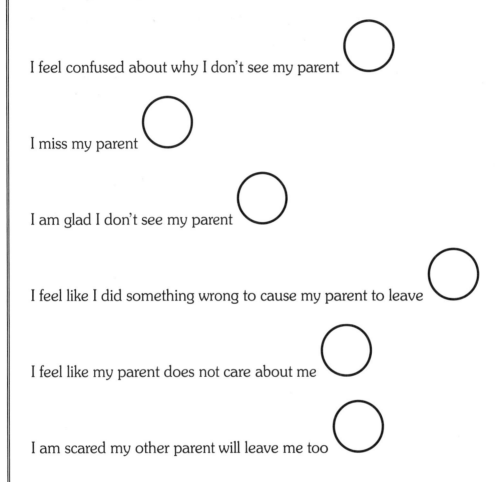

I feel confused about why I don't see my parent

I miss my parent

I am glad I don't see my parent

I feel like I did something wrong to cause my parent to leave

I feel like my parent does not care about me

I am scared my other parent will leave me too

Whatever you are feeling, know that your thoughts and reactions are normal. When a parent stops seeing his or her child, it is because that parent has problems to work out. These problems keep them from being an involved parent. These problems have nothing to do with anything you did. You may feel as though this parent doesn't care about you — that is not necessarily true. Your parent is missing out on a lot by not being close with you. And remember that even though you are not seeing one of your parents, you still have another parent to take care of you and love you!

Something for Your Feel Better Bag: The Shoulder Scrunch

You can help yourself feel better by relaxing your body. One way to relax your body is to do *The Shoulder Scrunch*. To do it, scrunch your shoulders up to your ears, then relax them and move them around until all the tightness and tension is gone. Do *The Shoulder Scrunch* a few times until your body feels relaxed. Add these instructions to your *Feel Better Bag*. Do *The Shoulder Scrunch* when you feel tense or upset and it will help you relax.

My Parents are Dating

When your mother and father are dating other people, you may experience many different feelings. You may feel happy that they have met someone else they like. You may feel sad because you want your parents to be together, instead of being with someone else. You may feel jealous of the time your parents are spending with their new adult friends. You may feel nervous being with this new person. All your feelings are normal. Circle the feelings you have about your parent dating. You can circle more than one feeling to show all the feelings you have. Add any other feelings you have that are not shown below.

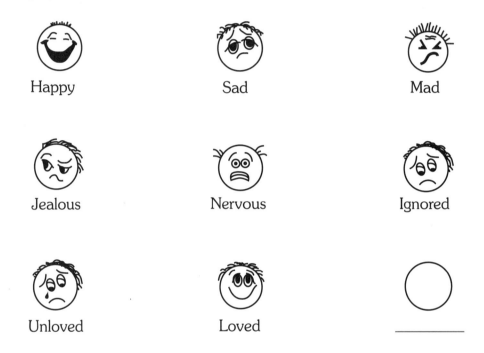

Happy   Sad   Mad

Jealous   Nervous   Ignored

Unloved   Loved   _____

If your parents are dating, you may feel like you do not get to spend enough time with them. It's important to let your parents know how you feel. You can write a letter to them. Below is an example.

Dear Mom/Dad,
I know you enjoy being with your girlfriend/boyfriend, but I miss spending time alone with you. Could you and I do something together each week that's just the two of us? That will help me feel better.
Love,

_____

It is important for you to know that if your parents are dating and start to like or even love the people they are dating, their love for you does not stop. Your parents still love you, no matter what!

Something for Your Feel Better Bag:
Hug Coupon

When you are feeling upset, you can ask your parent for a hug. Cut out the *Hug Coupon* below and, next time you are feeling upset, give it to your parent to let him or her know that you need a hug!

I need a hug!

My Parents are Getting Remarried

Your mother or father or both may get remarried. If a parent gets remarried, you will have a stepparent, and maybe stepbrothers, stepsisters, and new aunts, uncles, cousins, and grandparents. You may have to move, change schools, and adjust to a new way of life at home. You will experience many different feelings as your family goes through these changes. Below are some common reactions children have when their parents remarry. Read each statement and color in the circle to show how you feel. If you feel that way a lot, color in the whole circle. If you feel that way a bit, color in part of the circle. If you don't feel that way at all, leave the circle blank.

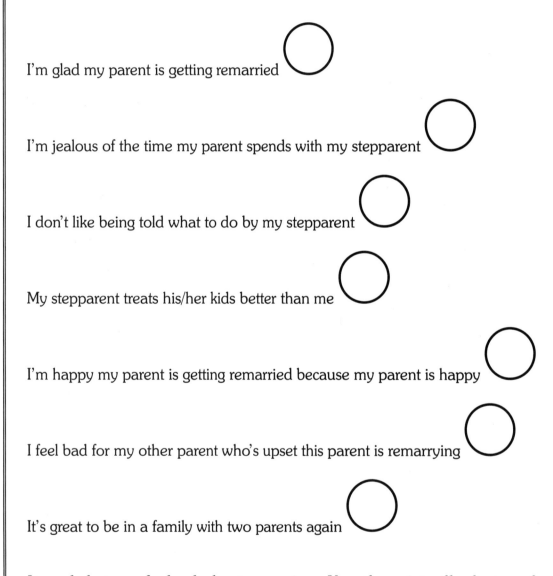

I'm glad my parent is getting remarried

I'm jealous of the time my parent spends with my stepparent

I don't like being told what to do by my stepparent

My stepparent treats his/her kids better than me

I'm happy my parent is getting remarried because my parent is happy

I feel bad for my other parent who's upset this parent is remarrying

It's great to be in a family with two parents again

It can help to read a book about remarriage. Your therapist will select one for you to read and talk about together.

Something for Your Feel Better Bag: Laughter Makes Me Feel Good
(Supplies: Comic section from the newspaper)

Laughter helps us feel good. Read the comics from the newspaper, think of a funny joke, or remember a funny moment. Laughing won't take your troubles away, but it will help you feel better for awhile.

Basketball: A Game about Divorce

(Supplies: Basketball hoop and basketball, or use crumpled paper and a garbage can)

It can be hard to talk about divorce, so let's play a special version of the basketball game to make it easier. To play, take turns shooting a basket. If you successfully throw the ball through the basketball hoop, you get two tokens. If you miss the basket, answer one of the questions below. You get one token for each question you answer. At the end of the game, trade in tokens for prizes: 1-10 tokens = 1 prize, 11 or more tokens = 2 prizes.

-1- **What is marriage?**
-2- **What is divorce?**
-3- **What is one reason** **parents divorce?**
-4- **What can children do or say** **when their parents argue** **in front of them?**
-5- True or false: **If a parent keeps missing visits** **with his or her child, it means** **they don't love the child**
-6- True or false: **Children often feel uncomfortable** **talking about divorce**
-7- True or false: **Once parents divorce they hardly** **ever get back together**
-8- True or false: **Talking to a therapist helps children** **understand and cope better** **with their problems**
-9- True or false: **Children must pick sides and** **love one parent more** **than the other**
-10- True or false: **If parents start arguing at their** **child's birthday party, the child** **should politely say "Please stop."**
-11- True or false: **If a child doesn't like the person** **his parent is dating, he** **should be mean to him or her**
-12- True or false: **When a parent says mean things** **about the other parent, the child** **should agree with them**

Answers to Basketball Game

Question #1: What is marriage?
Answer: When two people decide to become husband and wife.

Question #2: What is divorce?
Answer: When a husband and wife decide they no longer want to be married.

Question #3: What is one reason parents divorce?
Answer: Some reasons are: They were fighting a lot and couldn't make up; they couldn't fix their problems; they weren't happy being together anymore; they fell in love with someone else; they stopped being in love.

Question #4: What can children do or say when their parents argue in front of them?
Answer: They can politely say to their parents, "It upsets me when you argue, please stop" or they can go to another room, or they can say to themselves, "Even when my parents argue, they still love me."

Question #5: True or false: If a parent keeps missing visits with his or her child, it means they don't love the child.
Answer: False. When a parent misses visits, it is because that parent has problems that have nothing to do with love for his or her child. That parent still loves his or her child very much.

Question #6: True or false: Children often feel uncomfortable talking about divorce.
Answer: True. It can be hard to talk about sad things like divorce, but talking about it is a good way to get the feelings out.

Question #7: True or false: Once parents divorce they hardly ever get back together.
Answer: True. Once parents divorce it is usually forever.

Question #8: True or false: Talking to a therapist helps children understand and cope better with their problems.
Answer: True. Talking to a therapist will not solve all your problems but it can help make things better.

Question #9: True or false: Children must pick sides and love one parent more than the other.
Answer: False. Children don't have to pick sides; they can love both their parents.

Question #10: True or False: If parents start arguing at their child's birthday party, the child should politely say to them, "Please stop."
Answer: True. This is a good way for a child to handle this situation.

Question #11: True or false: If a child doesn't like the person his or her parent is dating, he or she should be mean to him or her.
Answer: False. It is normal for children to be upset when their parent starts dating, but even if the child doesn't like the person, it is not okay to be mean to him or her. It is better for children to talk to their parent about their feelings.

Question #12: True or false: When a parent says mean things about the other parent to the child, the child should agree with them.
Answer: False. A better way to handle this is for the child to politely say to the parent, "It upsets me when you say mean things about each other. Please stop."

Section 6

Interventions to Process
Emotional and Behavioral Reactions

The activities in this section are focused on processing emotional and behavioral reactions to the divorce. Sadness, anger, and guilt are common emotions experienced by children of divorce. Many children of divorce experience physical distress. Some children express their emotional distress by acting out. The games, expressive arts activities, and stories in this section address these common emotional and behavioral reactions.

Interventions

Ali and Her Mixed-Up Feeling Jar: *Ali's Story* helps children explore and discuss their feelings related to the divorce. Children can identify with Ali, and they can share in her experiences vicariously. Children's sense of isolation about the divorce may be reduced as they realize that other children, even if they are only fictional characters, have been through similar circumstances. As an alternative to coloring a jar, colored sand can be used to fill a jar.

My Body Doesn't Feel Good: Children of divorce may be experiencing physical distress in the form of headaches, stomachaches, tiredness, or difficulties eating or sleeping. It is helpful to normalize these physical reactions and convey the message that physical symptoms usually dissipate when feelings are more openly expressed.

Feeling Sad: Many children experience intense sadness regarding their parents' divorce. Some children may not feel they can cry, or they may not have permission to do so. This activity facilitates the expression of sadness and gives children permission to emote freely and openly.

Feeling Angry: Anger is a common emotion experienced by children of divorce. They may be angry at themselves if they feel responsible for the divorce, angry at a parent whom they blame for the family break-up, or angry at the circumstances following the divorce, such as having to move and/or switch schools. They may be internalizing their anger by being depressed or socially withdrawn, or they may be externalizing it by acting out aggressively. Whether children internalize or externalize anger, they need to learn healthy ways to express and cope with their strong emotions. This activity facilitates cathartic release and teaches anger management strategies. In order for these strategies to be most effective, children should be encouraged to practice newly-learned skills outside the therapy session. For this reason, the homework exercise is an important component to this activity. Whenever possible, include the parents in the session (or at the end of the session) so they can learn and model the anger management techniques and coach children between sessions. Some children will need additional sessions focused on the safe expression of anger before they are ready to learn anger control. If using this activity in group therapy, group members can have a play dough-pounding contest with one another.

Feeling Like It's My Fault/Getting Rid of Guilt: Young children are egocentric and often believe that they have caused the events that affect them. As a result, children may believe they caused the divorce. The issue of self-blame for the divorce is complex and multidimensional. The key to understanding self-blame lies in determining the child's belief system regarding why the divorce occurred. Children may wonder whether their misbehavior or negative thoughts toward their parents contributed to the divorce. Or they may feel guilty for not somehow preventing the family break-up. *Getting Rid of Guilt* contains cartoon statements that reflect misconceptions children typically have about the reasons for the divorce, and counter-statements to correct these misconceptions and to relieve feelings of guilt. Blank word-bubbles are included so the child can make up his or her own cartoons.

Getting Into Trouble: When children feel overwhelmed by strong negative emotions, they may act out to express their distress, or they may engage in negative attention-seeking behavior in order to elicit care. This activity can help children develop insight into this behavior in order to facilitate positive change.

Heads or Tails Feelings Game: Because this game touches on the various issues that were addressed in this section, it helps the child integrate the material. The game captures the interest of children and helps them verbalize their thoughts and feelings. The active component of the game (the *Tails* list) helps to channel the child's energy into positive outlets.

Ali and Her Mixed-Up Feeling Jar
(Supplies: Assorted colored crayons)

Children dealing with divorce usually have lots of mixed-up feelings inside. This activity will help you talk about your feelings. Read *Ali's Story,* then answer the questions below:

How did Ali feel at first when she was told her parents were getting a divorce?

What were some of Ali's worries?

Why did Ali feel guilty about the divorce?

How did Ali feel once she talked to her therapist about her feelings?

You may feel the same as Ali about your parents' divorce, or you may have different feelings. Think of how you feel about your parents' divorce, then make your own Feeling Jar by coloring the jar on page 105. Choose a different colored crayon for each feeling. Use more of one color to show feelings you experience a lot. Fill in the chart below to show the colors you chose for each feeling, and to explain your feelings about your parents' divorce.

Color	Feeling	Why I feel that way

Ali and Her Mixed-Up Feeling Jar

This is a story about a girl named Ali. Her parents got divorced. She has a lot of mixed up feelings inside her. She remembers the day her parents told her the awful news. Her mom and dad sat her down in the living room and her mom said, "Ali, you may have noticed that Daddy and I have been arguing a lot lately. We have some big grown-up problems. We tried hard to fix them, but we can't. So we have made a very big and difficult decision. We are getting divorced. Dad is moving out." At first Ali couldn't believe it. She was **shocked**! She thought her parents would make up and everything would be fine. But that didn't happen. Once Ali realized her parents were not getting back together, she felt so **sad**. But she pretended she was fine because she didn't want to make her mom more upset.

After her dad moved out, Ali **worried** that her mom would go away too. She was **scared** that there would be nobody left to take care of her. And since their money problems got worse after the divorce, Ali **worried** that they wouldn't be able to afford to send her back to summer camp.

Ali felt the divorce was her fault. She thought if she had been better behaved, her parents would still be together. This made Ali feel **guilty**.

Ali wondered if she should tell her friends about her parents' divorce. She felt **nervous** about what to say, and she **worried** that the kids at school would think her family was weird. But everyone at school found out anyway when her parents came to her school play and had a big argument in front of everyone, and her dad yelled at her mom, "It's a good thing we're divorced!" Ali felt so **embarrassed**!

Ali got **depressed** because her feelings were so mixed-up: **sad**, **guilty**, **worried**, **scared**, **embarrassed** — all these mixed-up feelings jumbled up inside her. Ali didn't know what to do with all these mixed-up feelings. So she pretended that she had a jar inside her stomach where she could keep all her mixed-up feelings. It wasn't a real jar of course, but Ali pretended to keep all her mixed-up feelings inside this jar.

Because of all the mixed-up feelings inside her, Ali sometimes did things she never used to, like get **angry** at people for no good reason. She threw toys around her room and yelled and screamed, even at her cat, Whiskers! Often, she had scary dreams that would wake her up in the middle of the night. When this happened, she would squeeze her teddy bear really hard and bury her head in her pillow until she fell back to sleep.

Even though her parents were divorced, the arguing didn't stop. Her parents argued when her dad came to pick her up for visits, and they argued on the phone. This **frightened** Ali. They told Ali she had to pick sides and decide which parent she wanted to live with. This made Ali feel **caught in the middle**. She loved them both and didn't want to have to choose one parent over the other. Ali felt so **confused**, more mixed-up feelings for her to stuff into the jar inside her stomach.

Ali wondered whether her parents still loved her. Maybe they stopped loving her, like they had stopped loving each other.

One night, while Ali's mother was putting her to bed, her mother said, "Ali, I love you very much. Your dad also loves you very much. We realized that it is not fair to make you choose sides, so we are going to make a plan so you can spend time with us both." This made Ali feel so **relieved**! For the first time in a long time, Ali felt **happy**. That night, she had a good dream and slept well.

The next week, Ali went to see a therapist whose job it was to help kids whose parents were divorced. At first, Ali felt **nervous** talking to the therapist, but after a while it got easier sharing her feelings. Ali even told the therapist about her pretend jar inside her stomach. As Ali began to talk more and more about her feelings, guess what happened? She began to feel better!

The end!

My Feeling Jar

Something for Your Feel Better Bag:
Coloring
(Supplies: Crayons)

Add some crayons to your *Feel Better Bag*. Next time you feel upset, let out your feelings by coloring a picture.

My Body Doesn't Feel Good
(Supplies: Band-Aids)

When you are upset, your body might feel upset too. You may feel more tired. You may have trouble eating or sleeping. You may have headaches or stomachaches, or other body pains. This activity will help you talk about how your body is feeling. Use the body outline below to put Band-Aids on the parts of your body that feel bad, hurt, or sick. Talk about your hurt with your therapist.

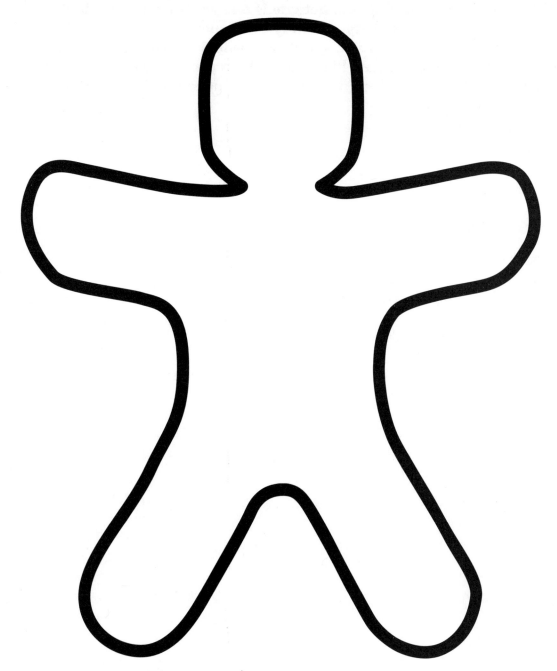

Keeping your feelings all trapped inside can make your body feel sick. Letting your feelings out can help your body feel better. Talking, writing, or drawing about your feelings are all helpful ways to help your body feel better.

Something for Your Feel Better Bag: Exercise

Doing a fun exercise or physical activity is one way to help your body feel better. Exercise and physical activity naturally bring more oxygen to the brain. That is why it can feel good to exercise and do a physical activity. Look at the list below and circle the ones you would like to do to help your body feel better. Add the list to your *Feel Better Bag*. Next time your body does not feel good, do one of the exercises from the list.

Do jumping jacks

Play music (not too loud) and dance around the room

Skip rope

Jog on the spot

Lie on the floor and stretch out your muscles

Play basketball with crumpled paper and a garbage can

Put a penny on the tip of your index finger and see how long you can walk around the room without it falling off

Add your own ideas: _____

Feeling Sad
(Supplies: A tissue, tape)

Everyone feels sad at times, but when parents divorce, it can make you feel saddest of all. When you feel sad, you may feel like crying. But you may be worried that if you cry, you will make others around you sadder. Or you may think that crying makes you seem weak or look like a baby. But crying is really a very strong and brave thing to do, and it is a good way to let out your hurt. If you don't feel like crying, that's okay too. Not everyone is a crier. This activity will help you talk about your sadness. Copy the questions on the next page onto a tissue, then write your answer to each question onto the tissue. When you are done, tape the tissue in the space below.

Questions about Sad Feelings

The divorce makes me feel sad because:

When I feel sad, I:

When I feel sad, I can get help by:

Something for Your Feel Better Bag:
Helping Myself When I Feel Sad
(Supplies: Mini tissue packet, scissors, glue, stickers)

It is normal to feel sad when parents divorce. Below is a list of things that might help you feel better when you are sad. Choose one of the ideas below (or write your own idea), cut it out, and paste it onto a mini tissue packet. Then decorate the tissue packet with the stickers. Add it to your *Feel Better Bag* as a reminder that you can help yourself feel better when you feel sad. If you ever feel like crying, you can use the tissues from your tissue packet.

Things I can do when I feel sad:

Ask someone for a hug

Cuddle a stuffed animal

Talk to an adult about my feelings

Do a favorite activity

Remind myself my parents still love me

Remind myself I won't always feel so sad

Feeling Angry
(Supplies: Play dough, Ziploc bag)

Anger is a common feeling children experience when parents divorce. There are many reasons why you may feel angry. You may keep your anger in or you may let your anger out by yelling, hitting, or throwing things. It's important to let your anger out in safe ways. Safe anger means you are not hurting yourself or anyone else when you are expressing your anger. A safe way to let out angry feelings is to pound play dough. (You can make your own play dough by following the recipe on the next page.) Pound the play dough as hard as you can for one minute without stopping. (If you'd like, you and your therapist can have a play dough-pounding contest and see who can pound the dough the hardest and longest!) As you continue to pound the play dough, tell about why you feel angry. (Have your therapist write your angry list in the space below as you pound the play dough.) Pound the play dough hard to show how angry you feel!

Think about your parents' divorce and fill in the sentences below:

I am angry because _____

I am angry at _____

It's not fair that_____

Below are some ideas for handling anger in safe ways. Choose one of the ideas from the list and use your play dough to sculpt something that represents the technique. For example, sculpt a Stop Sign for the "Visualize a Stop Sign" technique.

-Visualize a stop sign as a reminder to STOP before I lose control
-Slowly count backward from 20 until I feel calm
-Take slow deep breaths until my body feels relaxed
-Talk to an adult about my feelings
-Other ideas:

Put your play dough sculpture in a Ziploc bag. Take it home and add it to your *Feel Better Bag*. **It can remind you to use your new technique when you get angry.**

Recipe for Play Dough

(Supplies: Bowl, spoon, measuring cup, flour, salt, oil, water, food coloring, Ziploc bag, garbage bags, tape)

Tip: Tape garbage bags on and under the table to prevent mess.

Play Dough

In a medium size bowl, mix together the following:

2 cups of flour

½ cup of salt

2 tablespoons of vegetable oil

Gradually add ½ cup of water and mix together well.

If you need more water, add it a little bit at a time.

Add food coloring to the play dough

(you may want to divide the play dough into several clumps first,

so you can make different colors of play dough).

To keep the play dough soft, place it in a plastic Ziplock bag.

HOMEWORK

(Fill in this section at the end of the session)

Today I learned to handle my anger by: _____

My play dough sculpture will help me remember to: _____

I can practice this technique at home by: _____

My parent can help me practice by: _____

··

(Fill in this section at home and bring it to your next session)

Situation that made me angry: _____

Safe anger technique used: _____

How this technique helped me: _____

Feeling Like It's My Fault

Lots of children think they caused the divorce, even if they have been told it wasn't their fault. They may think they did something bad to make their parents divorce. Or they may think they should have done something to stop the divorce. Or there may be another reason why they feel guilty about the divorce. Fill in the sentences below to show how you are feeling:

I think my parents' divorce is my fault because:_____

_____

My parents would still be together if I would have:_____

_____

I feel bad because after my parents split up, I:_____

_____

I feel badly that I:_____

_____

Getting Rid of Guilt
(Supplies: Scissors, glue, markers)

When parents divorce, children often feel guilty about it. The word "guilty" means feeling bad for something we think we did wrong. The cartoons on the next pages are about children who feel guilty because of their parents' divorce. These children received some helpful words of advice from other children to help them get rid of their guilty feelings. Read the cartoons, then answer the questions below. Once you have answered the questions, color in the cartoons, cut them out, and staple the pages together to make a comic book. There are blank cartoons so you can add your own.

What are some reasons why children blame themselves for divorce?

What words of advice helped the children in the cartoons get rid of their guilt?

Have you ever felt guilty for your parents' divorce? If yes, why did you feel guilty?

What words of advice can you give yourself to help get rid of your guilt?

Remember: the divorce is not your fault. It doesn't matter what you did or didn't do. It doesn't matter what you said or didn't say. It doesn't matter if your parents had fights about you. Children are never to blame for divorce. Divorce happens because of problems between moms and dads, not because of anything a child does or thinks or says.

118

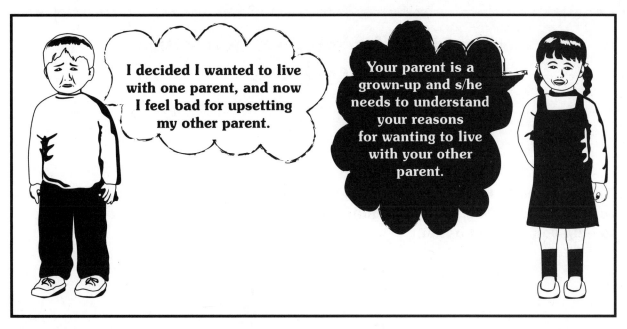

Something for Your Feel Better Bag: Secret Message

Break the code to uncover the secret message below. Then put the message in your *Feel Better Bag*. Whenever guilty feelings creep back in, look at the message to help yourself feel better.

A = 1	N = 14
B = 2	O = 15
C = 3	P = 16
D = 4	Q = 17
E = 5	R = 18
F = 6	S = 19
G = 7	T = 20
H = 8	U = 21
I = 9	V = 22
J = 10	W = 23
K = 11	X = 24
L = 12	Y = 25
M = 13	Z = 26

Example:

3 1 20 = CAT

BREAK THIS CODE:

14 15 20 8 9 14 7   9   19 1 9 4   15 18   4 9 4

3 1 21 19 5 4   20 8 5   4 9 22 15 18 3 5

(See answer on the next page)

Answer to the Secret Code

Nothing I said or did
caused the divorce

Getting Into Trouble

Children usually feel upset when their parents divorce, and they may start doing things or acting in ways they never used to. Sometimes children get into more trouble. Read the situations below, then answer the questions at the bottom of the page:

My parents divorced and I feel very angry. I get into fights with other kids and I'm mean to my little sister. I get into trouble at school and have to go to the principal's office. Last night my mom wouldn't let me watch TV so I threw the remote control at her and told her I wished she was dead. Later I felt bad about what I said. (Jason, age 7)

I started stealing around the time my parents separated. When I got caught stealing a chocolate bar, my mom got very angry and wouldn't let me play outside for a week. I stopped stealing for a while but then started doing it again after my mom started dating someone. I know it's wrong to steal, but I can't seem to stop doing it. (Beth, age 10)

I started wetting the bed after my parents separated. It isn't something I do on purpose, it just happens. One time I wet the bed when I was sleeping at my grandma's house. I was too embarrassed to tell her I wet the bed so I dumped water on the sheets and told her I accidentally spilled some water. Then I got into trouble for telling a lie. (Danny, age 9)

How do you think the children in each of the above situations feel?

Why do you think children sometimes get into more trouble after their parents divorce?

What advice would you give to each of the children in the above situations?

When children get into trouble a lot, they begin to feel that they are bad or no good. But it is important for children to understand that even if their behavior is bad, it does not mean that they are bad. Make a list of some things that are good, special, and lovable about you. Next time you begin to feel that you are a bad person, remind yourself that you are precious and lovable!

Something for Your Feel Better Bag:
Write About My Feelings
(Supplies: Pencil)

When children get into trouble a lot, it's usually because they're upset and can't talk about their feelings. But when children start to talk more and more about what's really bothering them, they eventually feel better and their behavior improves. Add a pencil to your *Feel Better Bag*. Next time you are upset, use the pencil to fill in the sentences below. Writing and talking about how you feel instead of getting into trouble will help you feel better about yourself.

I feel upset because:

Instead of getting into trouble I will calmly talk to _____ *about my feelings*

The Heads or Tails Feelings Game
(Supplies: A quarter, bag filled with small prizes)

Let's play a game about feelings. It is called *The Heads or Tails Feelings Game*. To play, take turns flipping a coin. If the coin lands on heads, answer a question from the *Heads* list below. If the answer is correct, get 2 tokens. If the coin lands on tails, follow the instructions from the *Tails* list below, then get one token. At the end of the game, trade in tokens for prizes: 1-10 tokens = 1 prize, 11 or more tokens = 2 prizes.

Heads

1. Name three feelings children have when their parents divorce.
2. True or false: It is best to keep feelings inside rather than to talk about them.
3. True or false: If a child is being hurt, s/he should tell a trusted adult.
4. True or false: Some children get stomachaches or headaches when they feel upset.
5. True or false: Some children misbehave more after their parents get a divorce.
6. What are some reasons why children may blame themselves for their parents' divorce?
7. True or false: Many children wish their parents would get back together.
8. Name three safe ways to express anger.
9. True or false: Children shouldn't cry if they feel sad because it makes them look like a crybaby.
10. What can you do to feel better when you are upset?

Tails

1. Hop to the other end of the room and back on one foot.
2. Show what happy looks like with your face and body.
3. Spin your body around five times, then try to touch your nose with your thumb.
4. Show what sad looks like with your face and body.
5. Jump up and down ten times.
6. Show what angry looks like with your face and body.
7. Do ten jumping jacks.
8. Show what scared looks like with your face and body.
9. Stomp your feet ten times.
10. Show what proud looks like with your face and body.

Answers to The Heads or Tails Feelings Game

1. **Name three feelings children have when their parents divorce.** Children experience many different feelings when their parents divorce, such as sad, scared, worried, confused, angry, guilty, lonely, and relieved.

2. **True or false: It is best to keep feelings inside rather than to talk about them.** <u>False</u>. It is important to find at least one person to talk to about your feelings. Talking about feelings usually helps people feel better.

3. **True or false: If a child is being hurt, s/he should tell a trusted adult.** <u>True</u>. If a child is being hurt by a parent, another adult, or another child, s/he should always tell another adult (even if s/he has been told to keep it a secret), so s/he can get help and the hurting can stop.

4. **True or false: Some children get stomachaches and headaches when they feel upset.** <u>True</u>. When people are upset, their bodies are upset too, and so they may get more stomachaches and headaches. When children talk about their upset feelings, it helps them feel better.

5. **True or false: Some children misbehave more after their parents divorce.** <u>True</u>. Sometimes children misbehave after the divorce because they feel so upset. They find it hard to talk about their upset feelings so they show they are upset by misbehaving. But when children start to talk more about what's bothering them, they usually feel better and their behavior improves.

6. **What are some reasons why children blame themselves for their parents' divorce?** There are many reasons why children think they made the divorce happen. For example, they may think they made their parents argue and that's why they got divorced. Or they may think they should have done something to make their parents stay together. But divorce is never a child's fault.

7. **True or false: Many children wish their parents would get back together.** <u>True</u>. Many children wish their parents will get back together, but chances are, once parents get a divorce, they stay divorced.

8. **Name three safe ways to express anger.** There are many ways to express anger in safe ways, such as visualizing a stop sign, slowly counting backwards, taking slow deep breaths, and talking to an adult about angry feelings.

9. **True or false: Children shouldn't cry if they feel sad because it makes them look like a crybaby.** <u>False</u>. It is normal and okay to cry when we feel sad.

10. **What can you do to feel better when you are upset?** There are many ways we can help ourselves feel better when we are upset. For example, we can write or draw about our feelings, or talk to someone.

Section 7

Interventions to Enhance Coping and Self-Esteem

Many children use maladaptive strategies to cope with their difficulties. If children do not learn healthy ways to cope, they are at risk for developing serious difficulties, such as depression, anxiety, or anti-social behavior. A number of interventions in this section focus on enhancing coping strategies.

Divorce and ongoing parental conflict can damage a child's self-esteem. Some children have such profound self-esteem deficits that they have internalized the belief that they are bad and their future is hopeless. Enhancing self-esteem for these children is not easy, yet it is essential in helping children to be resilient and able to cope with adversity in life. Activities from this section are designed to improve children's self-esteem and encourage a positive view of their futures. In order to strengthen a child's self-concept, parents must be part of the process, and must be coached how to positively interact with their children and foster their children's unique talents. The activities in this section will be significantly enhanced by working in conjunction with parents.

Interventions

Feeling Good About Myself/Feel Good Messages/I Deserve To Be Happy and Enjoy Life: These activities help children focus on their strengths and abilities, promote feelings of self-worth, encourage a more optimistic attitude, and instill a message of hope for the future. These are important therapeutic goals for children of divorce, and help set them on a path toward strength and healing. If using the *Feeling Good About Myself* activity in a group, have one balloon/balloon message for each group member. (If there are more than eight group members, add additional questions to the game.)

I Can Have a Happy Marriage Someday: Many young people from divorced families develop a negative attitude toward marriage, or worry that they may repeat the marital failure they experienced in their own families. Moreover, if children grew up in a family with little positive interaction between their parents, then they may not have a realistic sense of marital intimacy and love. This activity enables children to explore the elements that create a happy marriage and instills hope regarding positive intimate relationships in the future.

Coping with Bad Dreams: Many children of divorce suffer from nightmares. If nightmares are interfering with the child's daily functioning, this activity can be used in the earlier stages of therapy. If a pillowcase cannot be obtained, have the child write or draw the coping strategy on a piece of paper to take home and keep by his or her bed.

The Coping with Divorce Game: This game helps children integrate the many concepts addressed throughout the interventions in this book. It facilitates the child's problem-solving abilities, which is an important goal in the final stages of therapy. If using this game in a group, have one question for each group member. If there are more than six group members, add additional questions to the game.

Giving a Helping Hand: This intervention can be used in the termination phase of therapy to provide children with the opportunity to offer words of advice to other children. Helping others is empowering and healing for the child.

What I Learned: This activity is for use at the end of therapy. It helps children review and evaluate their experiences in therapy. To prepare the activity, select a small gift appropriate to the client; for example, a small stuffed animal, or bottle of bubble bath. The gift can also be a graduation certificate, or the child's scrapbook. The gift should be wrapped in five layers of different colored wrapping or tissue paper so that each time the child answers one of the five questions on the worksheet, s/he gets to unwrap one layer of the gift.

Looking At This Book: This activity should be done in the second to last session. It helps the child review achievements in therapy, and prepares the child to share his or her scrapbook with his or her parents. If the child chooses to share the book with parents, it is best to have a separate session with the child and each parent. It is also suggested that the practitioner meet with the parents ahead of time to prepare them to respond appropriately to the child and the material in the scrapbook.

Feeling Good About Myself:
The Balloon Bounce Game
(Supplies: 6 balloons, pen)

Today we are going to talk about self-esteem. Self-esteem means how you feel about yourself. If you have good feelings about yourself, it means you have high self-esteem. You can help yourself have high self-esteem by thinking about the good things, like things you do well and your proud moments. *The Balloon Bounce Game* **will help us talk about these good things. To play, blow up six balloons and knot each one. Write one question from the list below onto each balloon. Now, together with your therapist, try to keep two balloons up in the air for one minute without them touching the ground. Then catch a balloon, read the question written on it, and take turns answering the question. Repeat until all questions have been answered. At the end, you can burst the balloons!**

Questions

What's something you are proud you can do?

Tell about a time you were able to do something difficult.

Tell about a time you felt proud of yourself.

Tell about a time you were nice to someone.

Tell about a time you helped yourself feel better.

Say something nice to someone else in the room.

Something for Your Feel Better Bag:
My Proud Moment
(Supplies: Balloon)

Fill in the sentence below:

Something I did that I'm especially proud of _____

_____

Put a balloon in your *Feel Better Bag*. Next time you are feeling upset, blow up the balloon, knot it, and bounce it in the air without letting it touch the ground for as long as you can. As you are bouncing the balloon, think about your proud moment that you wrote about in the space above.

Coping with Bad Dreams
(Supplies: White pillowcase, fabric markers)

Everyone has bad dreams sometimes. In the space below, draw a picture of a bad dream you have had recently:

Below are things you can do to help yourself when you wake up from a bad dream. Choose one of the strategies and write or draw it on a pillowcase. Take the pillowcase home and put it on your pillow or next to your bed. Next time you wake up during the night from a bad dream, the pillowcase will remind you to use your strategy!

Say to myself: It's not real, it's just a dream

Think of a better ending to the dream

Imagine my favorite superhero fighting off the scary monsters

Hug my pillow or stuffed animal until I feel calm and safe

Think about a happy memory

Ask my parent to sit by my bed until I fall asleep

I Deserve To Be Happy and Enjoy Life!

You have been through a difficult time since your parents divorced, and you may have stopped doing things you enjoy. It may be hard for you to play, laugh, or have fun now, but you can—and you deserve to. You deserve to be happy and enjoy life! Draw or write about some things you like doing.

Make a plan to do something you enjoy this week. If it's something that you used to do when your parents were together, you can feel good about the happy memories you have!

Something for Your Feel Better Bag: Thinking Good Thoughts

Next time you are feeling upset, try this strategy: Close your eyes and think about the things you enjoy doing. Let the happy feelings spread through your body. Just thinking about the things you enjoy doing can bring you happiness!

I Can Have a Happy Marriage Someday
(Supplies: Happy face stickers, adult male and female figurines or puppets)

Children in divorced families may worry about getting married someday because they may fear they will get divorced just like their parents. But it is important to know that lots of people have happy marriages and never get divorced. You can have a happy marriage someday! Below is a list of some things that can make a happy marriage. Put a happy face sticker beside each one. If you'd like, you can add your own ideas to the list.

They spend fun time together

They help each other

They treat each other nicely

They talk to each other and work out their problems

They hold hands, hug, and kiss

They love each other

Other things that make a happy marriage: _____

Use the people figurines or puppets to make up a skit to show what a happy marriage looks like, or write a play about a happy marriage.

Something for Your Feel Better Bag:
I Can Have a Happy Marriage
(Supplies: Happy face sticker)

Add a happy face sticker to your *Feel Better Bag* as a reminder that you can have a happy marriage someday.

Feel Good Messages
(Supplies: Scissors, glue, colored paper, decorating materials)

Going through a divorce is sad and difficult, but there are things you can do to make it easier. Reading *Feel Good Messages* is one way you can help yourself feel better. Read the *Feel Good Messages* below, cut out the ones you find helpful and glue them onto a poster board. You can make up your own *Feel Good Messages* if you'd like. Decorate your poster and add it to your *Feel Better Bag*. Read the poster to yourself whenever you need help and comfort.

I can help myself feel better when I'm upset

I can feel good about my proud moments

I made it through tough times before and I can make it through tough times now

My parents divorced each other but they didn't divorce me

I don't need to worry about fixing my parents' problems

It wasn't my job to save my parents' marriage

Nothing I said or did caused the divorce

I don't have to take sides; I can love both my parents

I am special and lovable

I can be happy for all that I have

I don't have to take care of my parents—they can take care of themselves

I deserve to be happy and enjoy life

Parents who get divorced still love their kids!

The Coping with Divorce Game
(Supplies: Bag filled with small prizes)

This game will give you some ideas on how to cope better with divorce. To play the game, take turns reading the questions below and circling the best answer. (Correct answers are on the next page.) If the answer is correct, pick something from the Prize Bag. Continue playing until all the questions have been answered.

(1) Abdul feels angry that his parents got a divorce. Circle the best way for him to cope with this problem:
(a) He should take out his anger by punching his little brother
(b) He should pretend he feels fine and hope his anger goes away
(c) He should express his anger by talking to an adult who will listen to his feelings

(2) William's parents tell him mean things about each other. Circle the best way for him to cope with this problem:
(a) He should agree with his parents when they tell him mean things about each other
(b) He should politely say, "Please stop saying mean things about each other"
(c) He should blast the radio to drown out anything his parents say

(3) Kim hates going back and forth between her mother's home and her father's home. Circle the best way for her to cope with this problem:
(a) She should keep a toothbrush, pajamas, and a special toy at each of her parent's homes
(b) She should refuse to visit her father because it's too difficult to go back and forth
(c) She should tell her parents they have ruined her life

(4) Robbie thinks he is to blame for his parents' divorce because he was always getting into trouble and his parents were always fighting about him. Circle the best way for him to cope with this problem:
(a) He should feel guilty for causing the divorce
(b) He should act perfect so his parents will love him
(c) He should tell himself his parents didn't divorce because of anything he said or did

(5) Brad does not like his father's girlfriend and he is jealous of the time his father spends with her. Circle the best way for him to cope with this problem:
(a) He should be mean to the girlfriend so she will stay away
(b) He should talk to his father about how he feels
(c) He should refuse to see his father until he dumps his girlfriend

(6) Mitasha's parents get into arguments a lot and yell and scream at each other. Circle the best way for her to cope with this problem:
(a) She should yell and scream too and tell her parents she learned this behavior from them
(b) She should get involved and try to stop the arguments
(c) She should politely say, "Please stop fighting in front of me"

Answers to The Coping with Divorce Game

1(c): Anger is a common feeling children experience when parents divorce. Talking to an adult about angry feelings is a healthy way to express anger.

2(b): It hurts when children hear their parents say mean things about each other. Children can stand up for themselves by politely asking their parents to stop doing this.

3(a): Keeping a set of essential items at each parent's place, as well as a special toy will make it easier to go back and forth between the two homes.

4(c): Children often think the divorce was their fault. But it is important for children to know that parents do not divorce because of anything a child does or says, they divorce because of grown-up problems.

5(b): It is normal for children to feel jealous of the time a parent spends with a boyfriend or girlfriend. The best way to cope with these feelings is to talk about it. But if children find it too difficult to tell their parents their true feelings, they can find someone else to talk to, like a therapist or a relative.

6(c): It is normal for parents to get into arguments with each other, whether they are divorced or not. But it can be difficult for children to hear their parents argue. Children can politely ask their parents to stop fighting in front of them. If their parents are hurting each other, children should tell a trusted adult.

What I Learned
(Note to therapist: See Overview for Practitioners for activity preparation)

Congratulations! You have reached the end of this book. That means you have done a lot of hard work and have learned many things about divorce. Answer the questions below to review your thoughts and feelings. For each question you answer, you get to unwrap a layer of the gift. Answer all the questions to get to the gift!

You did many different activities in therapy. Which activities helped you most?

You learned a lot about divorce. What are some things you learned?

Children have feelings about ending therapy. Some children feel happy to end therapy, some children feel sad or upset about ending therapy. How do you feel about ending therapy?

You have made it through a difficult time. What do you think about yourself now that you have made it through such a difficult time?

You have learned many ways to help yourself through tough times. What are some ways you can help yourself feel better when you are upset in the future?

Giving a Helping Hand

You have learned a lot about dealing with divorce and you can give a *helping hand* to others. Trace an outline of your hand in the space below, and on the inside of the hand write a helpful message to other children who are dealing with divorce:

My Feel Better Bag:
My Favorite Strategies

Now that you are ending therapy, your *Feel Better Bag* should be filled with things to help you feel better. Go through your bag and choose some things that have helped you the most. Whenever you are feeling upset, you can use the different ideas from your *Feel Better Bag* to help yourself feel better!

My favorite strategies from my *Feel Better Bag*:

1. _____

2. _____

3. _____

Looking At This Book

This book is a very special book because it contains your hard work. Go through your book and see all that you have accomplished. As you go through your book, answer the following questions:

Which activities did you like best?

Which activities were the hardest?

Which activities helped you most?

You will have a chance to show your book to your parents when you come here the last time. Look through your book and choose what you want to show them. You can show them your whole book, parts of the book, or not show it at all. You get to decide what you want to show and what you want to keep private.

You can take this book home if you want to when you come here the last time. Talk with your therapist about where to keep it at home so it is in a safe, private place. Or it can be kept here in the office in a locked place, and you can come get it when you are ready. When you look at this book now and when you are older, it will help you remember all the hard work you did. It will also remind you that you made it through a tough time, and that is something to really be proud of!

Section 8

Interventions for Group Sessions

Children dealing with divorce can benefit greatly from participating in group therapy. The group setting provides a developmentally appropriate environment in which children can share their thoughts and feelings about the divorce. Group therapy offers the following advantages:

- Allows assessment of child's functioning: The group becomes a microcosm of society so it allows the therapist to gain insight into the children's presentation in their everyday lives.
- Promotes universality: Allows children to see that they are not the only ones living in a divorced family. This counters elements of secrecy, isolation, and the sense of "being different."
- Facilitates vicarious learning: Children observe the expressions of fellow group members and learn from others.
- Encourages greater risk-taking and catharsis: Children who are initially cautious to explore and express certain issues may open up as they see other peers engage in activities.
- Enhances interpersonal skills: Children have the opportunity to interact with peers and master new behaviors.

Ethical and Legal Considerations

There are a number of ethical and legal considerations that practitioners must adhere to when facilitating groups for children of divorce:

- The practitioner must have proper training and supervision in group therapy with children of divorce.
- Group leaders should be covered by Professional Liability Insurance.
- Written consent for the child's participation in group must be obtained from all legal custodians.
- In the event that a child discloses abuse during group, proper channels for reporting must be followed.
- Group leaders should adhere to standards of practice regarding record-keeping.
- Participant contract ensuring group confidentiality and group rules should be secured at the start of the first session.
- A clinical file should be kept on each group member and a copy of each activity placed in the file.

Group Leadership

Effective group leadership is essential to creating a safe and caring therapeutic environment. If the group is run by co-leaders, they must model respect for one another, agree on roles and the structure and content of the group, and have compatible beliefs about how to work with children of divorce. A skilled clinical supervisor can assist co-leaders in developing a good working relationship.

Group Composition

Consideration must be given to the group composition. In terms of size, groups for children of divorce should be kept fairly small in order to best respond to the emotional and behavioral needs of the children. Four to eight members with two leaders is optimal. The group can be mixed genders with an appropriate balance of girls and boys. The age range of the members should generally not exceed twelve months. Some children are not group-appropriate. Ginott (1961) suggested the following contraindications: (1) Extremely aggressive children; (2) Sexually acting-out children; (3) Children with serious psychiatric disturbances; (4) Siblings who exhibit intense rivalry. Decisions regarding group composition must be based on maximizing the children's sense of safety and positive clinical experience.

Assessment and Screening

Each child should be assessed individually to determine his or her clinical needs and if the group is the most appropriate treatment modality. The assessment interventions in Section Four can be used as part of this assessment, along with the Parent Questionnaire in Section Three. If possible, a teacher report should be obtained to further clarify the child's functioning. If the child participated in a group before, the group leader should determine whether the child managed well in that situation.

Group Structure and Content

The length and number of sessions can vary, but generally groups for younger children should be shorter, given their limited attention span, i.e. 45-60 minutes, and groups for school-aged and adolescent clients, 60-90 minutes.

Each session should adhere to a similar structure so the group members know what to expect. It can be helpful to begin each session with a check-in ritual, to assess current functioning and facilitate self-expression. For example, each child can point to a feeling face on a chart to indicate how s/he is feeling. A quick ice-breaker game can then be played. There are many excellent resources containing group ice-breakers, such as *Games for Group* (Cavert 1999) and *Quicksilver* (Rohnke and Butler, 1995). Next, the group members can complete the divorce-specific treatment activity or activities planned for the session. (The group leader should be prepared to divert from the planned activity if needed.) While the interventions in this section have been designed specifically for use in group counseling, many interventions from this book can be modified for the group format. A *Sample Group Curriculum* has been included, to give an idea of group structure and content. A fun closing activity can be initiated to help end the session on a lighter note. An energetic closing activity to appropriately channel excess adrenalin caused by anxiety can be helpful.

Sample Group Curriculum

The following are suggested interventions for a ten-week group for children of divorce, ages 7-12. Each group member should be assessed and screened prior to group and, if needed, provided with individual and/or family therapy, as an adjunct to group counseling. In addition to the interventions listed below, each session should begin with an ice-breaker, and end with a fun and energetic closing activity. Each group member should be given a scrapbook in the first session, and all their activities should be placed in this book (see *Guidelines* in Section One). A session with each child and his or her parent(s) should be scheduled at the end to provide feedback and treatment recommendations.

Session #1: Getting Acquainted
Goals: (1) Establish group rapport and cohesion (2) Define the purpose of the group and rules
Interventions: (1) Welcome Letter (2) Decorate scrapbook cover (3) About Me (4) Balloon Bounce

Session #2: Understanding Divorce
Goals: (1) Verbalize an understanding of divorce (2) Increase comfort level talking about divorce
Interventions: (1) Marriage and Divorce Puzzle (2) Divorce: How It Works (3) Scavenger Hunt

Session #3: Identifying & Expressing Feelings
Goals: (1) Normalize and identify feelings associated with divorce
Interventions: (1) Ali and Her Mixed-Up Feeling Jar (2) Group Card Game

Session #4: Sharing Stories
Goals: (1) Share circumstances of the divorce (2) Express thoughts & feelings regarding divorce
Interventions: (1) My Parents' Divorce (2) Read and process the book, *I Don't Want to Talk About It* (Ransom)

Session #5: Living in Two Houses
Goals: (1) Express thoughts and feelings toward parents (2) Implement adaptive coping strategies for transitions between two homes
Interventions: (1) Spending Time with My Mother and Father (2) Luggage Tag

Session #6: Expressing and Coping with Sadness
Goals: (1) Identify and express sad feelings associated with the divorce (2) Verbalize an acceptance that parents will not reunite
Interventions: (1) Feeling Sad (2) I Wish My Parents Would Get Back Together

Session #7: Identifying and Expressing Anger
Goals: (1) Identify and express angry feelings associated with the divorce (2) Identify safe ways to express anger
Interventions: (1) Feeling Angry (2) Road Rage (Lowenstein, 2002, p. 64)

Session #8: Feeling Good About Myself and My Future
Goals: (1) Implement adaptive coping strategies (2) Verbalize positive thoughts regarding marriage
Interventions: (1) Feel Good Messages (2) I Can Have a Happy Marriage

Session #9: Coping with Divorce
Goals: (1) Implement adaptive coping strategies
Interventions: (1) Coping with Divorce Game (2) Paper Plate Puppet Shows

Session #10: Termination
Goals: (1) Review gains in counseling (2) Celebrate accomplishments made in counseling (3) Provide positive termination experience (4) Say goodbye to each other
Interventions: (1) Giving a Helping Hand (2) Pizza Party

Therapeutic Responses

Facilitating a group for children of divorce requires clinical skill. One important skill is to provide appropriate therapeutic responses to group members. Below are some examples:

Reflecting interaction: *"Johnny and Mike, you don't want to sit beside each other because you are still mad about what happened last session."*

Reflecting content: *"Sounds like everyone in the group wishes their parents were still together."*

Reflecting feelings: *"Johnny, you're really mad that your dad cancelled his last visit with you."*

Tracking behavior: *"Johnny, you are feeling angry so you are stomping your feet."*

Limit setting: *"Johnny, you're angry at Mike for calling you stupid, but it is not okay to hit Mike. Use your words to let Mike know you feel angry."*

Enlarging the meaning: *"Johnny, you feel like the divorce was your fault. Children often feel that way. Who else in the group feels like they are to blame?"*

Common Group Therapy Mistakes

Group therapy can be a powerful and therapeutic treatment modality for children of divorce. However, group facilitators can hinder the group process by making the following mistakes:

- Inadequately screening members for group appropriateness and readiness
- Facilitating mini sessions in group rather than utilizing the group
- Focusing on content more than process
- Not allowing the children to speak and work out issues together

Under the right circumstances, group therapy can be tremendously therapeutic for children of divorce. Being with other children in similar circumstances has the greatest power to normalize a child's experience.

Interventions

Balloon Bounce: It is helpful to begin a first group session with an ice-breaker. The *Balloon Bounce* activity helps group members get to know one another, and it facilitates communication and group cohesion. To prepare the activity, write a "getting acquainted" question onto each balloon. (Use a black permanent marker to write the questions onto the balloons to avoid smudging.) Examples of questions include:

What do you like to do for fun?
What's your favorite food?

What's a food you really hate?
What's your favorite movie?
What's your favorite game?
What makes you feel excited?
What's something that really bugs you?
When was the best day of your life?

The questions can be modified to suit the age and needs of the group. Suggested processing questions include: What new information did you learn about the members of the group? What did you discover about the things you have in common with other group members? How are you different from the others in the group? What is important about getting to know the others in the group?

Scavenger Hunt: This intervention promotes communication regarding divorce, catharsis of feelings, and problem-solving. It encourages creative thinking and open dialogue among group members. Copy the list of scavenger hunt items so each group has its own. A group leader should be assigned to each group to assist with reading and writing and to facilitate appropriate group interaction.

Group Card Game: This therapeutic game helps the group explore a number of treatment issues, including: (a) Defining marriage, divorce, and several other divorce-related terms; (b) Understanding why parents divorce; (c) Expressing feelings related to divorce; (d) Exploring feelings of guilt, sadness, and anger; (e) Resolving reunification fantasies; (f) Dealing with loyalty conflicts; and (g) Disengaging from marital conflict. The active component of the game (the *Action Cards*) helps to channel the children's energy into positive outlets. To prepare the game, copy each *Question Card* and *Action Card* onto separate index cards, or photocopy the *Question* and *Action Card* sheets onto colored card stock and cut out each card. (The questions can be adapted depending on the ages of the children and treatment needs of the group.) Place the *Question Cards* and *Action Cards* in two separate piles in the middle of the group. The *Guide* can be placed beside the question cards for easy reference during the game. At the end of the game, process the activity by asking each group member to identify something they learned about divorce.

Paper Plate Puppet Shows: Children's adjustment to divorce depends largely on how well the parents handle the situation. Unfortunately, many parents exacerbate children's distress by arguing in front of the child, asking the child to pick sides, or being inconsistent with visitation. This activity helps group members learn appropriate ways to handle these difficult situations.

Pizza Party: This activity can be used in a final group session as a creative way to affirm therapeutic gains, and to provide the opportunity to discuss the children's feelings about termination. The celebratory atmosphere that is created in the session facilitates a positive termination experience for the children. To prepare the activity, make a copy of the *Pizza Party* worksheet for each group member. Photocopy the puzzle onto colored card stock and cut along the dotted lines to make six cardboard pizza slices. Place the six cardboard pizza slices in a small bag. (Note: Obtain permission from parents to offer pizza to the children.)

Balloon Bounce: A Group Ice-Breaker Game

(Supplies: One balloon per group member and leader, black permanent marker)

This game will help us get to know one another. It is called *Balloon Bounce*. Each group member will get a balloon. The balloons have questions written on them that will help us get to know one another. At the count of three, we will throw the balloons in the air and try to keep them in the air without them touching the ground. When I yell "Stop!" everyone will let the balloons fall to the ground. One group member will be chosen to pick up a balloon and answer the question. Everyone will get a chance. Once everyone has answered the question, we will throw the balloons back into the air and play another round. The game will continue until we have answered all the questions on the balloons.

Scavenger Hunt
(Supplies: Paper, markers)

You will be divided into two teams. Each team will get a list of items to collect. You will have 15 minutes to collect as many items on the list that you can. The team that collects the most items from the list wins.

Scavenger Hunt Items

Definition of divorce

3 feelings children may have when parents divorce

Something blue

A picture of the group leader(s)

2 people with the same shoe size

3 safe ways to express anger

Outline of a hand

Words of advice to help children who feel the divorce was their fault

Something that can help children of divorce

A group of children holding hands and singing a song

The Group Card Game
(Supplies: Deck of playing cards, cookies)

Divorce can be hard to talk about, so let's play a card game to make it easier. To play, take turns picking the top card from the stack of cards. If you get a card with an even number (2,4,6,8,10), pick a *Question Card* and answer the question. If you do not feel you can answer the question, you can ask the group for help. If you get a card with an odd number (3,5,7,9), pick an *Action Card* and follow the instructions. If you pick an ace, skip a turn. If you pick a jack, do 10 jumping jacks. If you pick a queen or king, you get a cookie. At the end of the game, everyone who played gets a cookie.

Guide

Even cards = Question card

Odd cards = Action card

Ace = Skip turn

Jack = Do 10 jumping jacks

Queen, King = Get cookie

Question Cards:
The Group Card Game

(1) What is marriage?	**(2) What is divorce?**	**(3) What are some reasons why parents divorce?**
(4) What are some feelings children may have when parents divorce?	**(5) How do you think children feel when they see their parents argue?**	**(6) Why do children sometimes hide their sad feelings?**
(7) What are some changes that happen at home after divorce?	**(8) True or false: Children sometimes blame themselves for the divorce**	**(9) True or false: Some children feel relieved when their parents divorce**
(10) True or false: Once parents divorce they hardly ever get back together	**(11) What is custody?**	**(12) What is visitation?**
(13) What is child support?	**(14) True or false: If parents argue, the child should politely say, "Please stop"**	**(15) True or false: If a child is being hurt, he or she should tell an adult**
16) True or false: A parent should try to win their children's love by buying them expensive gifts	**(17) True or false: After divorce, children may worry they won't be taken care of**	**(18) True or false: Children must pick sides and love one parent more**
(19) What can a child do if his parents argue at his birthday party?	**(20) True or false: A child who misbehaved a lot is to blame for the divorce**	**(21) True or false: When a parent says mean things about the other, the child should agree**
(22) What is a safe way to handle angry feelings?	**(23) True or false: It is up to children to save their parents' marriage**	**(24) True or false: Parents who get divorced still love their kids**

Answers:
The Group Card Game

1) What is marriage? When two people decide to become husband and wife.

2) What is divorce? When a husband and wife decide they no longer want to be married, they get a legal ending to their marriage.

3) What are some reasons why parents divorce? There are many reasons why parents divorce, for example: they were fighting a lot and couldn't make up; they tried to fix their problems but couldn't; they weren't happy being together anymore; they stopped being in love; they fell in love with someone else; they decided their marriage was a big mistake.

4) What are some feelings children may have when parents divorce? Children may experience many different feelings when parents divorce, such as sad, angry, guilty, worried, confused, embarrassed, relieved.

5) How do you think children feel when they see their parents argue? Children may feel scared, sad, worried, or angry when they see their parents argue.

6) Why do children sometimes hide their feelings? Children may hide their feelings because they don't want others to know they are upset. But it is important for children to find at least one person they can talk to about their true feelings.

7) What are some changes that happen at home after divorce? Divorce can bring many changes at home, such as: one parent moves out, the family has to move, children go back and forth between two homes, children may have new jobs or chores to do.

8) True or false: Children sometimes blame themselves for divorce. True. Children may feel like the divorce was their fault. They may feel they said or did something to make it happen. But divorce happens because of problems between grown-ups, not because of anything a child does or says.

9) True or false: Some children feel relieved when their parents divorce. True. Children may feel relieved when their parents divorce, especially if the fighting between their parents stops after the divorce.

10) True or false: Once parents divorce they hardly ever get back together. True. Once parents divorce it is usually forever.

11) What is custody? A legal word for the parent who is in charge of taking care of the children and making the big decisions like where the children will live and go to school.

12) What is visitation? A schedule of when children will see or stay with each of their parents.

13) What is child support? Money one parent gives to the other to help pay for the things the children need.

14) True or false: If parents argue, the child should politely say, "Please stop." True. Children can politely say to their parents, "It upsets me when you argue, please stop."

15) True or false: If a child is being hurt, he or she should tell an adult. True. Children should tell an adult if they are being hurt, so they can get help and the hurting can stop.

16) True or false: A parent should try to win their children's love by buying them expensive gifts. False. Parents cannot make children love them more by buying them expensive gifts.

17) True or false: After divorce, children may worry that they won't be taken care of. True. But children should know they will be taken care of after divorce. Their parent will care for them and, if needed, other adults can help care for the children.

18) True or false: Children must pick sides and love one parent more than the other. False. Children don't have to pick sides; they can love both their parents.

19) What can a child do if his parents argue at his birthday party? The child should politely say to them, "Please stop."

20) True or false: A child who misbehaved a lot is to blame for the divorce. False. Children may feel their misbehavior caused the divorce. But divorce does not happen because of anything a child did; divorce happens because of problems between grown-ups.

21) True or false: When a parent says mean things about the other parent the child should agree. False. The child should politely say, "Please do not tell me anything mean about my other parent."

22) What is a safe way to handle angry feelings? Safe anger means expressing anger in a way that does not hurt yourself or anybody else. Some safe ways to express anger are: talking to an adult, walking away, helping your body to feel calm and relaxed.

23) True or false: It is up to children to save their parents' marriage. False. It is not up to children to save their parents' marriage. It is up to the parents to handle their problems.

24) True or false: Parents who get divorced still love their kids. True! Parents who get divorced still love their children no matter what! Parents' love for their children is forever love.

Action Cards:
The Group Card Game

Hop to the other end of the room and back on one foot	Spin your body around five times then try to touch your nose with your thumb	Switch seats with someone in the group
Jump up and down ten times	Shake hands with someone in the group	Give someone in the group a high-five
Do ten jumping jacks	Switch seats with the person sitting to your left	Give a high-five to the person sitting to your left
Give a high-five to the person sitting to your right	Switch seats with the person sitting to your right	Stomp your feet ten times
Touch your toes	Shake hands with the person sitting to your left	Stand on your toes for five seconds
Take five slow deep breaths	Shake hands with the person sitting to your right	Give yourself a hug

Paper Plate Group Puppet Shows
(Supplies: Paper plates, tongue depressors or popsicle sticks, markers)

The group will be divided into groups of three. Each group will get a situation card and must create a puppet show to perform in front of the rest of the group. The puppet shows are about problems children may have whose parents are divorced. Each group will perform two puppet shows; the first showing an inappropriate way to handle the problem, and the second showing an appropriate way to handle the problem. Each puppet show must have a beginning, middle, and end. Make a paper plate puppet for each character in the puppet show, i.e. child, mother, father.

Situation cards

Problem: Parents have an argument at their child's birthday party
Inappropriate solution: Child tells parents they ruined his/her birthday
Appropriate solution: Child politely says to parents, "This is <u>my</u> special day. Please stop arguing."

Problem: A parent arrives very late to pick the child up for a visit
Inappropriate solution: Child refuses to go on the visit
Appropriate solution: Child calmly tells parent how he/she feels, "It upsets me when you arrive so late."

Problem: A parent tells a child he has to choose to live with him or her
Inappropriate solution: Child chooses to live with one parent and refuses to see the other parent
Appropriate solution: Child tells parents, "Please don't make me pick sides; I love you both."

Problem: A parent asks the child questions about the other parent
Inappropriate solution: Child shouts, "It's none of your business!"
Appropriate solution: Child politely says, "Mom/Dad, it makes me feel uncomfortable when you ask me about the other parent. Please stop."

Problem: A child feels jealous of the time his or her parent is spending with his/her new girlfriend/boyfriend
Inappropriate solution: Child acts mean toward his or her parent's girlfriend/boyfriend
Appropriate solution: Child tells parent, "I feel sad that we don't spend much time together. Can we do something together each week, just you and me?"

Pizza Party
(Supplies: Small bag filled with the cardboard pizza slices, dice, transparent tape, pizza)

Today we are going to honor and celebrate the progress you made in this group by playing a party game. To do that, each of you will complete a worksheet, and then we are going to play a game called *Pizza Party*. At the end of the game, we get a special treat!

(Distribute a *Pizza Party* worksheet for each group member to complete. Once the worksheets have been completed, group members sit in a circle with their completed worksheets in front of them. The bag filled with the six puzzle pieces is placed in the middle of the circle.)

We will now play *The Pizza Party Game*. To play, we will take turns rolling the dice and answering the question on the worksheet that matches the number on the dice. For example, when a player rolls 2, that player shares his or her answer for question number 2 on the worksheet ("The group activity that helped me the most"). All players then share their answer for question 2. The player who rolled the dice then draws a cardboard pizza slice from the bag. Each cardboard pizza slice represents an item for a pizza. All six cardboard pizza slices must be earned in order to complete the pizza puzzle. The game is played until all six numbers of the dice have been rolled and each of the six questions on the worksheet has been answered. If during the game, a player rolls a number that has already been used, the player rolls again until a new number comes up. When all the questions have been answered and the six cardboard pizza slices have been earned, the group will put the cardboard pizza puzzle together. The group is then awarded a special treat: pizza!

Worksheet
Pizza Party

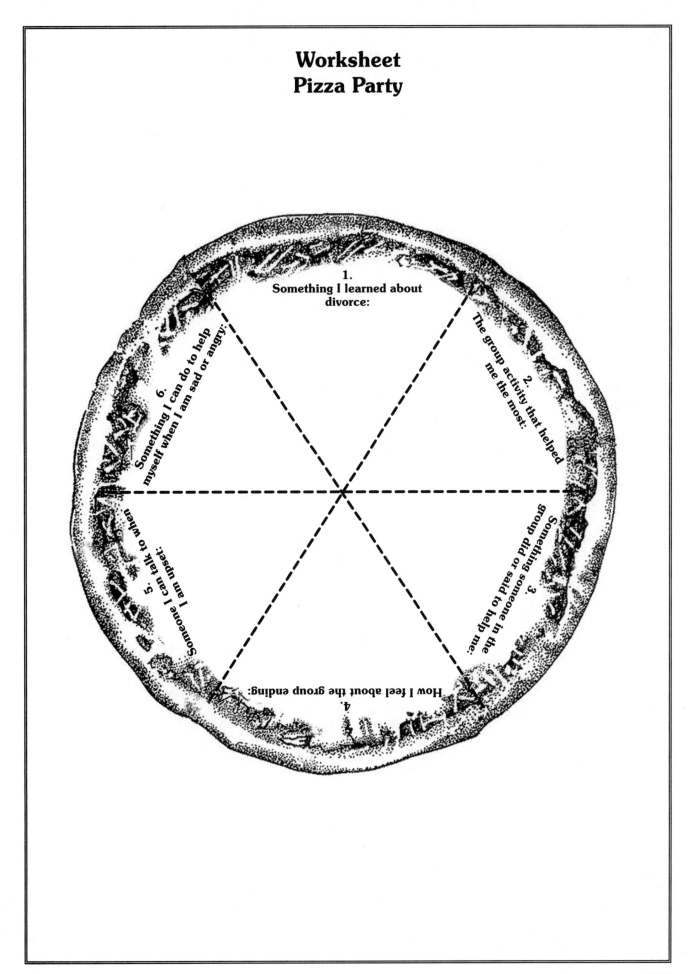

1.
Something I learned about divorce:

2.
The group activity that helped me the most:

3.
Something group did or someone in the group did or said to help me:

4.
How I feel about the group ending:

5.
Someone I can talk to when I am upset:

6.
Something I can do to help myself when I am sad or angry:

Pizza Party Puzzle

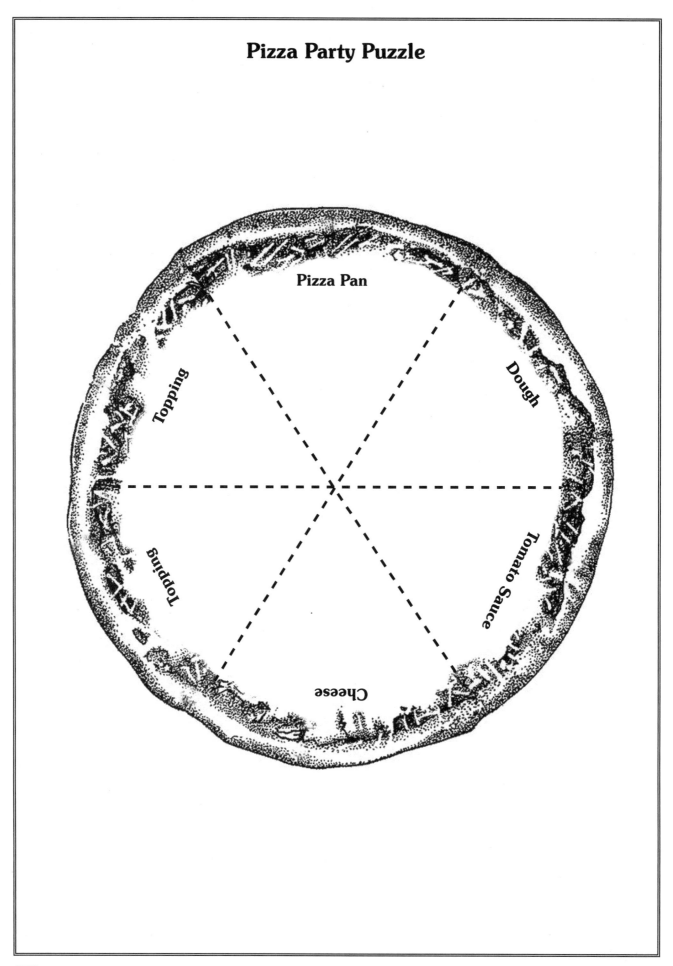

Section 9

Interventions for Family Sessions

Conducting family sessions as part of the treatment process for children of divorce is highly beneficial to both the child and the family. Treatment goals for divorced families include:

• Facilitating ongoing open and honest communication about the divorce and other salient issues
• Educating the parents about the impact of divorce on children
• Helping the child to communicate unmet needs to the parents
• Helping the parents to support one another's role in the child's life
• Establishing a consistent routine that is followed in both homes

Rationale for Use of Play in Family Therapy

Play-based interventions can be incorporated into family sessions. Gil (1994) outlines the following benefits for using play in family therapy:

• Provides a comfortable medium for children
• Engages family members in a common, pleasurable task
• Facilitates a broad scope of diagnostic information
• Unlocks a deeper level of communication
• Exposes underlying thoughts and feelings
• Encourages family relatedness

This section includes a number of play-based family interventions, namely, art, games, and storytelling.

Role of the Family Therapist

The role of the family therapist is to:

• Engage all family members
• Facilitate the activities
• Assess family dynamics
• Model new patterns and skills
• Offer interpretations that will facilitate healthy family functioning
• Discuss how family play activities can be integrated into home settings

The practitioner can meet with the parent(s) ahead of time to explain the importance of family involvement in therapy, and to preempt the family's resistance to engaging in the play activities by conveying the expectation that the family will benefit from this technique.

When working with divorced families, the practitioner must decide whether it is best to meet with the child and both parents together, or to alternate sessions with the child and each of his or her parents.

In some cases, it is not appropriate for the same therapist to provide both the individual counseling to the child as well as the family therapy. Some children need the undivided support and advocacy of the therapist. In these circumstances, it is best for the therapists (one for the child and one for the parents/family) to work collaboratively. The therapists must take care not to become polarized or caught in the unhealthy dynamics of the family conflict.

Interventions

The Family Gift: It is helpful to assess the family dynamics that contribute to the child's functioning and adjustment. Evaluating children within the context of their family can provide useful clinical information that assists in the development of treatment goals. Infants and toddlers should be included in the session, even though they are too young to directly participate in the activity. The practitioner uses *The Family Gift* technique to assess the following family dynamics: a) Who makes the decisions? b) How well can the parent organize without over-controlling? c) Can the parent encourage the child's ideas rather than imposing his or her own? d) Which member's suggestions were utilized and which were ignored? e) Were they able to negotiate and reach consensus? f) Who made friendly gestures and who made hostile gestures? g) Did the interaction take on a structure, or was it chaotic? h) What was the level of affect? i) Was the parent able to set appropriate limits and offer appropriate praise and affection? j) If there is more than one child, can the parent appropriately attend to the needs of each child? k) Did any dysfunctional patterns emerge, i.e. parentification, triangulation, disengagement, scapegoating, overfunctioning? l) Who engaged in the activity and enjoyed the play?

The Family Card Game: This is a useful diagnostic and treatment tool. It enables the family to communicate more openly and have a shared understanding of the divorce, strengthens support between parent and child, and facilitates healthy coping. To prepare the game, copy each question from the list provided onto separate index cards, or photocopy the question card sheet onto colored card stock and cut out each question. (The questions can be adapted depending on the ages of the children and the treatment needs of the family.) At the end of the game, process the activity by asking the family what they learned about one another and about divorce.

A Typical Day: It can be difficult for children to transition between two homes, particularly if they must adjust to different sets of rules and routines. This intervention enables the family to establish and abide by one routine, and to set rules and consequences so there is greater consistency in both homes. Since both parents must be willing to adhere to similar rules and routines, parental cooperation should be established prior to completing this activity with the child and parents.

Postcards: Children often have difficulty expressing their feelings and needs to their parents. This intervention helps to open the lines of communication between parents and children about difficult issues. It gives children the words to express their thoughts and needs, and it guides parents to respond appropriately. It is suggested that the practitioner meet with the parents, prior to involving the child in the session, to review the content of the postcards, and prepare them to respond in a sensitive manner.

Play Date/Nightly Snuggle: Children need comfort and attention from their parents, yet many parents have difficulty providing their children with these basic needs, particularly parents in the midst of divorce who may be preoccupied with their own distress. These interventions promote ways for parents to attend to their children's need for physical affection and quality time. If the relationship between a parent and child is strained, the parent will need additional guidance from the therapist on how to engage the child. The therapist can also help the parent and child plan the activities for their play date, preempt potential problems, and debrief with them shortly after the time spent together.

The Family Gift

(Supplies: Gift bag, craft supplies such as markers, tape, cardboard, popsicle sticks, pipe cleaners, etc.)

This activity is called *The Family Gift*. Create a gift for your family using any of the supplies provided. It should be a gift that everyone in the family wants. It can only be one gift, and you must all agree what the gift should be and how it might be used in your family. Once you have created your gift, place it in the gift bag. You have 30 minutes to decide and create your gift.

When you are done (or the 30 minutes is up) answer the questions below:

Describe your gift

Tell how you each felt as you were deciding and creating your gift

Who made the decisions? For example, who decided what the gift should be?

Were two or more people in your family able to cooperate and work well together?

Did anyone cause any difficulties or disagreements and, if so, how was this handled?

Is there anything about the way you did the activity that reminds you of how things work in your family at home?

How can the gift help your family? What else can help your family?

The Family Card Game
(Supplies: Deck of playing cards, cookies)

This game will help your family talk together about the divorce. To play, take turns picking the top card from the deck of cards. If you get a card with an even number, pick a card from the *Question Card* pile and answer the question. If you get a card with an odd number, pick a card from the *Question Card* pile and ask someone in your family to answer the question. The *Question Cards* will help you talk about how things are in your family, your feelings about the divorce and ways you can cope with your feelings. If you do not feel you can answer the question, you can ask your family for help. If you pick an ace, ask someone in your family for a hug. If you pick a jack, do 10 jumping jacks. If you pick a queen or king, you get a cookie. At the end of the game, everyone who played gets a cookie.

Guide

Even cards = You answer

Odd cards = You choose a family member to answer

Ace = Ask for a hug

Jack = Do 10 jumping jacks

Queen, King = Get cookie

Questions
The Family Card Game

Tell three feelings you have had since the divorce	**Tell about a worry you have had since the divorce**	**Tell about a fun time you have had with your family**
What are some reasons why people divorce?	**How do you think children feel when they see their parents argue?**	**What would you say to someone who thought they should hide their sad feelings?**
Tell something that is different at home since the divorce	**Why do you think some children blame themselves for divorce?**	**What is something you would like to change about your family?**
Share a special memory of something you did together as a family	**Who do you think is the happiest in your family and why?**	**What is something you are looking forward to doing?**
Who do you think is the saddest in your family and why?	**What is something you can do that would be helpful for your family?**	**Tell about a new chore or job you have in your family since the divorce and how you feel about it**
What advice would you give a child who felt he was not getting enough attention?	**What should a child do if he misses a parent while visiting his other parent?**	**What advice would you give a child who felt she had to pick sides and love one parent more?**
How do you think a child feels if his parents argue at his birthday party?	**Tell about your best day ever**	**What is something parents can do to help their child when they are upset?**
What is a healthy way to express angry feelings?	**Tell about a time someone in your family did something nice for you**	**Tell about a time you felt proud of yourself**
What helps you feel better when you are upset?	**What is something you can do to make things better in your family?**	**What do you appreciate the most about your family?**
Make up your own question	**Make up your own question**	**Make up your own question**

A Typical Day

It can be hard for children in divorced families to go back and forth between two homes. One way to make it easier is for families to establish and follow the same routine at both homes. This activity will help your family establish a routine that is based on your child's needs. Together with your child, fill in the following schedule, have two copies made, and put it on the fridge at each home. It may not be possible to follow the schedule everyday, but do your best to follow it whenever possible.

Child's Morning Routine

Wake up time: _____ Routine: Brush teeth, get dressed, other:_____

Eat breakfast: My favorite breakfast foods are: _____

Make lunch: My favorite lunch foods are: _____

Leave for school at: _____

Child's After School Routine

Arrive home at: _____

Have a snack. My favorites are: _____

Complete homework.

This is where I will do homework at Mom's:_____

This is where I will do homework at Dad's:_____

Complete chores.

Chores to do at Mom's: _____

Chores to do at Dad's: _____

Playtime. What I like to do for fun:_____

Dinnertime at: _____ My favorite foods for dinner are:_____

Child's Bedtime

Bed time: _____ Routine: Change into pajamas, brush teeth, other:_____

At bedtime I like to (circle what you like): Snuggle with my parent, talk with my parent about my day, have my parent read me a bedtime story, get tucked into bed.

Rules and Consequences

Some rules at Mom's and Dad's for me to follow:

1._____

2._____

3._____

If I break the rules, Mom or Dad will: _____

Family Time

What I like to do with Mom: _____

What I like to do with Dad: _____

Postcards
(Supplies: Postcards, colored markers)

Sometimes it can be hard for children to talk to their parents about their feelings or needs. Writing it down can make it easier. Below are some examples of feelings and needs children may have. Copy each one onto a postcard and decorate them (the parent can do the writing and the child can do the decorating). Take the postcards home and decide together where to keep them so they can be used when needed.

Dear Mom/Dad,
I feel upset and need to talk to you.
Love,
_____
PS: Please write back.

Dear Mom/Dad,
I feel ignored or left out and need more attention from you.
Love,
_____
PS: Please write back.

Dear Mom/Dad,
Someone is hurting me but I'm afraid to tell you about it.
Love,
_____
PS: Please write back.

Dear Mom/Dad,
It upsets me when you argue or tell me bad things about each other. Please stop.
Love,
_____
PS: Please write back.

Dear Mom/Dad,
I think the divorce was my fault. Is that true?
Love,
_____
PS: Please write back.

Dear Mom/Dad,
I'm worried if I love my other parent it will make you sad. Is this true?
Love,
_____
PS: Please write back.

Postcards Tip Sheet (For parents)

Take this tip-sheet home in case you need guidance on how to respond to your child.

Child: I feel upset and need to talk to you.
Parent response: I am here to listen. You can tell me anything.

Child: I feel ignored or left out and need more attention from you.
Parent response: Let's plan some special time together, just you and me.

Child: Someone is hurting me but I'm afraid to tell you about it.
Parent response: Please tell me so I can help make the hurting stop. You can tell me anything and I won't be mad at you.

Child: It upsets me when you argue or tell me bad things about each other. Please stop.
Parent response: Thank you for reminding me. I will do my best to stop.

Child: I think the divorce was my fault. Is that true?
Parent response: Nothing you did, said, thought, or felt made the divorce happen. The divorce happened because your dad/mom and I weren't happy being together anymore.

Child: I'm worried if I love my other parent it will make you sad. Is this true?
Parent response: It's okay for you to love us both.

Play Date

To Parents:
Children benefit from special one-on-one time with their parents. Parents and children can have regular "play dates," in which they spend time playing and interacting with one another. This special time has three parts: planning, doing, and evaluating.

<u>Planning</u>
Decide with your child what you will do together for your play date, and when you will do it. It need not be an expensive outing. Playing a board game, building a fort, or baking cookies are great ways to spend quality time together. You and your child can each suggest a few ideas for your play date, then let your child choose something from the list. It is best if it is something fun and interactive. Avoid activities that are competitive or that have little interaction like playing computer games or going to a movie. Plan the date and time and mark it on your calendar. If you have to cancel, be sure to reschedule to avoid disappointing your child.

<u>Doing</u>
Maintain a positive interaction during this special time with your child. This is not the time for criticizing or punishing. Only set limits if your child is doing something hurtful, otherwise, let it go! The activity you do is less important than the interaction, so be relaxed and playful, and give your child your undivided attention.

<u>Evaluating</u>
Talk with your child afterward about what s/he liked and disliked about the time spent together. If you'd like, you can use the evaluation below:

Evaluation of our Play Date

What we did together:_____

How we decided what to do:_____

Child's rating: I had a (circle one) bad/good/great time because:

Parent's rating: I had a (circle one) bad/good/great time because:

Plan a play date regularly with your child. Aim for at least thirty minutes once a week.

Nightly Snuggle

To Parents:

All children need comfort. But when parents divorce, children need extra comfort. The nightly snuggle is a ritual you can do with your child each night at bedtime. Snuggle with your child and ask him or her about his or her day, i.e. "Was your day terrible, okay, or great, and what happened to make it terrible, okay, or great?" If your child reports a terrible day, and you are not sure how to respond, here are some suggestions:

Repeat: You feel upset because…

Normalize: It's normal and okay to feel upset about…

Explore: Tell me more about your sad feelings

Praise: I'm glad you can talk to me about your feelings

Don't feel you have to make it all better. Just listening, validating feelings, and offering comfort is what your child needs from you.

Be consistent—have snuggle time every night you are with your child. Support the other parent's role by stating, "Tomorrow night you will be with your mom/dad and you will have snuggle time with her/him, because she/he loves you just as much as I do!"

Appendix A

Custody/Access Dispute Contract
(Adapted from the Court Clinic in Ottawa, Canada)

The purpose of this contract is to obtain written agreement that the therapist will not be asked to participate in any litigation regarding the custody/access dispute. If the therapist is asked to participate in litigation, the therapist's neutral role with the family may be compromised. This is likely to seriously jeopardize any progress that may have been made in therapy. In order to prevent such deterioration of any therapy, it is crucial that I/we have every reassurance that there will be absolutely no involvement on my/our part in current or future litigation between the parents. This is best accomplished by both parents signing this statement:

We wish to enlist the services of _____ in the treatment of
(name of agency or therapist)

our family. We understand that such treatment will be compromised if information

revealed therein is brought to the attention of the court in the course of a custody/access

dispute. Accordingly, we mutually pledge that we will neither individually nor jointly

involve _____ in any litigation whatsoever. We will neither
(name of agency or therapist)

request nor require _____ to provide testimony in court. If the
(name of agency or therapist)

services of a mental health professional are desired for court purposes, the services of a

person outside of _____must be enlisted.
(name of agency or therapist)

We have read the above, discussed these provisions with any attorney that we may be involved with at the present time and agree to proceed with the therapy.

_____   _____

Date   **Signature of parent**

_____   _____

Date   **Signature of parent**

_____   _____

Date   **Witness/(Therapist)**

Appendix B

Sample Graduation Letter

Dear Lisa,

I am writing you this letter to let you know how proud I am of you! You have worked so hard in therapy and you have made wonderful progress. I remember when you first came to see me. You felt very sad about your parents' divorce, but it was hard for you to talk about your feelings. We did many activities together to help you talk about your feelings. You especially liked playing Feelings Tic-Tac-Toe because you got candy at the end of the games! You've come a long way in being able to express yourself, and that's great progress!

We played a lot of games together, but the Air Hockey Game stands out as one of the games that I think really helped you a lot. I remember when we played the game, we talked about how hard it can be for kids to go back and forth between two homes. I'm glad the game gave you some helpful ideas to make it easier for you to go back and forth between your mom's home and your dad's home.

We spent many sessions dealing with guilty feelings. You talked about how you blamed yourself for your parents divorce, and how you wished you could have stopped your parents from splitting up. But your parents had grown-up problems that they couldn't fix and, even though they stopped loving each other, they both still love you very much.

Your parents also worked hard in therapy. They learned to stop arguing in front of you. They learned to stop telling you mean things about each other. And they learned to give you lots of snuggle time!

A few weeks ago, when we played the Balloon Burst Game, we talked about your proud moments, like when you got a good report card and when you won the art contest. I know that you will have many proud moments ahead of you, and you will be a shining star in whatever you choose to do!

You have already been through a lot in your young life, but your experiences have made you a stronger person. Always remember that you have made it through difficult times before, so you can make it through tough times ahead. And when you are having a tough time, you can use one of your favorite ideas from your Feel Better Bag, like The Spaghetti Technique, or writing in your special journal.

Lisa, I have enjoyed working with you. You have done a great job sorting out your feelings and talking about some very hard stuff. I wish you all the very best because you deserve it!
Best wishes,
Liana

Appendix C

TREATMENT PLAN FOR CHILDREN OF DIVORCE
(Adapted from *The Child Psychotherapy Treatment Planner*, Jongsma & Peterson)

Child to participate in individual and/or group therapy to address the following:

Verbalize positive feelings toward the therapist
-Therapist to actively build the level of trust with the client through active listening, unconditional positive regard, and warm acceptance
-Therapist to explore, encourage, and support the child in verbally expressing feelings regarding the divorce

Verbalize an understanding of divorce and express feelings related to the divorce
-Read books about divorce (see list of books in the resource section)
-Complete the following interventions: Feeling Faces Cut 'N Paste; Feelings Tic-Tac-Toe; My Parents' Divorce; How I Think, Feel and Behave; Butterflies in My Stomach; Marriage and Divorce; Divorce: How It Works; Changes in My Life; Caught in the Middle Scribble Game; Ali and Her Mixed-Up Feelings Jar; Feeling Sad; I Don't See My Parent Anymore; Sometimes My Parent Misses Visits; My Body Doesn't Feel Good; My Parents are Dating; My Parents are Getting Remarried; Heads or Tails Feelings Game; Basketball: A Game About Divorce

Implement adaptive coping techniques
-Use coping/self-soothing techniques through use of the Feel Better Bag
-Complete the following interventions: Going Back and Forth Between Homes Air Hockey Game; Luggage Tag; Getting into Trouble; Coping with Bad Dreams; Feel Good Messages; Coping with Divorce Game

Identify appropriate ways to deal with parental conflict
-Complete the following interventions: My Parents Argue and I Feel Stuck in the Middle; My Parents are Fighting Over Me

Verbalize an acceptance that parents will not reunite
-Complete the following intervention: I Wish My Parents Would Get Back Together

Express feelings of anger about the divorce through appropriate outlets
-Complete the following intervention: Feeling Angry
-Play Road Rage (from *More Creative Interventions for Troubled Children and Youth* by Lowenstein)
-Complete The Don't Flip Your Lid Anger Management Program (from *More Creative Interventions for Troubled Children and Youth* by Lowenstein)
-Parents to establish a reward system with the child to reinforce good anger control

Eliminate self-blame statements regarding the divorce
-Complete the following interventions: Feeling Like It's My Fault; Getting Rid of Guilt
-Each parent to write letter to child affirming s/he is not responsible for the divorce

Verbalize positive feelings toward both parents
  -Complete the following interventions: I Am Angry at My Parent; Billy's Story

Increase positive thoughts about self and future
  -Complete the following interventions: Feeling Good About Myself; I Deserve to be Happy and Enjoy Life

Verbalize hope regarding positive intimate relationships in the future
  -Complete the following intervention: I Can Have a Happy Marriage Someday

Express achievements in therapy and view termination as a positive process
  -Complete the following interventions: What I Learned; Giving a Helping Hand; Looking at this Book
  -Meet with parent(s) to prep for graduation ceremony and help them write letter to child for child's scrapbook
  -Therapist to write a graduation letter to child
  -Have a graduation ceremony

Family to participate in therapy to address the following:

Increase open communication in the family about the divorce
  -Complete the following intervention: Family Card Game
  -Each parent to hold regular meetings at home to allow children to express thoughts and feelings

Child to identify and verbalize unmet needs to parents
  -Complete the following intervention: Postcards

Parents to verbalize increased awareness of the effects of divorce on children
  -Read and discuss the handout, *Helping Your Children Through Separation and Divorce*
  -Read books about children and divorce (see list of books in the resource section)

Parents to provide child with consistent attention and nurturance
  -Complete the following interventions: Play Date; Nightly Snuggle

Parents cease making negative remarks about the other parent in presence of the children
  -Parents to actively participate in conflict-resolution counseling

Parents cease from obtaining information and/or sending messages to the other parent through the children
  -Parents to actively participate in conflict-resolution counseling

Resources

For Children
Dinosaurs Divorce: A Guide for Changing Families, by L. Krasny-Brown and M. Brown

How It Feels When Parents Divorce, by J. Krementz

I Don't Want To Talk About It, by J. F. Ransom

It's Not Your Fault, Koko Bear (Also available: Koko Bear Worry Doll), by V. Lansky

Was It The Chocolate Pudding? A Story for Little Kids About Divorce, by S. Levins and B. Langdo

Divorce is a Grown Up Problem, by J. Sinberg

Through the Eyes of Children: Healing Stories for Children of Divorce, by J.R. Johnston et al

Mom's House, Dad's House for Kids, by I. Ricci

I Know I Made It Happen (addresses feelings of guilt), by L. Blackburn

Brave Bart: A Story for Traumatized and Grieving Children, by C.H. Sheppard

Let's Talk About It: Stepfamilies, by F. Rogers

My Mother Got Remarried: And Other Disasters, by B. Park

Talk About It Divorce Cards, by J. Lane-Anderson; www.talk-aboutit.com

Mommy and Daddy are Fighting (domestic violence), by S. Paris

For Parents
Talking To Children about Divorce, by R. Garon and B. Mandell

Divorce Book for Parents, by V. Lansky

Helping Your Kids Cope with Divorce the Sandcastles Way, by M.G. Neuman

The Truth about Children and Divorce, by R.E. Emery

Mom's House, Dad's House, by I. Ricci

Parenting After Divorce, by P.M. Stahl

Two Happy Homes: A Guide for Divorced Co-parents and Stepparents, by S. Thomas

The Good Divorce, by C. Ahrons

Cooperative Parenting and Divorce, by S.B. Boyan and A.M. Termini

Divorce Poison, by R. A. Warshak

References and Suggested Readings

Alpert-Gillis, L.J., Pedro-Carroll, J.L., & Cowan, E.L. (1989). Children of divorce Intervention Program: Development, implementation, and evaluation of a program for young urban children. *Journal of Consulting and Clinical Psychology*, 57, 583-587.

Baris, M., Garrity, C. (1988). *Children of divorce: A developmental approach to residence and visitation.* PsytecCorp.

Baris, M., Coates, C., Duvall, B., and Garrity, C. (2001). *Working with high-conflict families of divorce: A guide for professionals.* New Jersey: Jason Aronson.

Barsky, A. (2004). *Clinicians in court: A guide to subpoenas, depositions, and testifying.* New York: Guilford.

Burroughs, M.S., Wagner, W.W., & Johnson, J.T. (1997). Treatment with children of divorce: A comparison of two types of therapy. *Journal of Divorce and Remarriage*, 27(3-4), 83-99.

Cavert, C. (1999). *Games (& other stuff) for group.* Oklahoma City: Wood & Barnes Publishing.

Clulow, C.F. (1990). Divorce as bereavement: Similarities and differences. *Family and Conciliation Courts Review*, 28(1), 19-22.

Crisci, G., Lay, M., and Lowenstein, L. (1997). *Paper dolls & paper airplanes: Therapeutic exercises for sexually traumatized children.* Indianapolis, IN: Kidsrights Press.

Gil, E. (1994). *Play in family therapy.* New York: Guilford.

Ginott, H. (1961). *Group psychotherapy with children: The theory and practice of play therapy.* New York: McGraw-Hill.

Hetherington, E.M., Stanley-Hagan, M., & Anderson, E.R. (1989). Marital transitions: A child's perspective. *American Psychologist*, 44, 303-312.

James, O. (1997). *Play therapy: A comprehensive guide.* Northvale, New Jersey: Jason Aronson.

Johnson, C.V., Riester, A.E., Corbett, C., Buehler, A., Huffacker, L., Levich, I., et. al. (1998). Group activities for children and adolescents: An activity group therapy approach. *Journal of Child & Adolescent Group Therapy*, 8(2), 71-88.

Johnston, J., & Campbell, L.E.G. (1988). *Impasses of Divorce: Dynamics and Resolution of Family Conflict.* New York: The Free Press.

Johnston, J., Breunig, K., Garrity, C., & Baris, M.A. (1997). *Through the eyes of children: Healing stories for children of divorce.* New York: The Free Press.

Johnston, J.,& Roseby, V. (1997). *In the name of the child: A developmental approach to understanding and helping children of high conflict divorce.* New York: Free Press.

Johnston, J., Walters, M., and Friedlander, S. (2001). Therapeutic work with alienated children and their families. *Family and Conciliation Courts Review.* 39(3) 316-333. (To order contact: www.blackwell-synergy.com)

Johnston, J. (2003). Parental alignments and rejection: An empirical study of alienation in children of divorce. *Journal of the American Academy of Psychiatry and the Law*, 31, 158-170.

Jongsma, A. (2002). *The child psychotherapy treatment planner.* Hoboken, NJ: Wiley.

Kelly, J. & Johnston, J. (2001) The alienated child: A reformulation of parental alienation syndrome. *Family and Conciliation Courts Review.* 39 (3), 249-266. (To order contact J. Kelly at 415-924-1407; email jbkellyphd@mindspring.com)

Kelly, J. (2002). Psychological and legal interventions for parents and children in custody and access disputes: Current research and practice. *Virginia Journal of Social Policy and Law*, 10 (1), 129-163. (To order contact J. Kelly at 415-924-1407; email jbkellyphd@mindspring.com)

Kelly, J. & Emery, R. (2003). Children's adjustment following divorce: Risk & resilience perspectives. *Family Relations*, 52: 352-362. (To order contact J. Kelly at 415-924-1407; email jbkellyphd@mindspring.com)

Kendall, P. (2000). *Childhood disorders.* East Sussex, UK: Psychology Press.

Kurdek, L.A., & Berg, B. (1983). Correlates of children's adjustment to their parents' divorce. In L.A. Kurdek (Ed.), *New directions in child development*: Vol. 19. Children and divorce, 47-60. San Francisco: Jossey-Bass.

Kurdek, L.A., & Berg, B. (1987). Children's beliefs about parental divorce scale: Psychometric characteristics and concurrent validity. *Journal of Consulting and Clinical Psychology*, 55, 712-718.

Lowenstein, L. (1995). The resolution scrapbook as an aid in the treatment of traumatized Children. *Child Welfare*. 74:4: 889-904.

Lowenstein, L. (1999). *Creative interventions for troubled children & youth*. Toronto, ON: Champion Press. (To order call: 416-575-7836 or www.lianalowenstein.com)

Lowenstein, L. (2002). *More creative interventions for troubled children & youth*. Toronto, ON: Champion Press. (To order call: 416-575-7836 or www.lianalowenstein.com)

McCarthy, G. (1998). Attachment representations and representations of the self in relation to others: A study of preschool children in inner-city London. *British Journal of Medical Psychology*, 71 (1), 57-72.

Oppawsky, J. (1991). The effects of parental divorce on children in West Germany: Emphasis: From the view of children. *Journal of Divorce and Remarriage*, 16(3-4), 291-304.

Pedro-Carroll, J.L., Sutton, S.E., & Wyman, P.A. (1999). A two-year follow-up evaluation of a preventive intervention program for young children of divorce. *School Psychology Review*, 28, 467-476.

Pedro-Carroll, J.L. (2001). The promotion of wellness in children and families: Challenges and opportunities. *American Psychologist*, 56, 993-1004.

Rohnke, K. and Butler, S. (1995). *Quicksilver*. Dubuque, Iowa: Kendall/Hunt Publishing Company.

Roseby, V., and Johnston, J.R. (1997). *High-conflict, violent, and separating families: A group treatment manual for school-aged children*. New York: The Free Press.

Sandler, I.N., Tein, J.Y., Mehta, P., Wolchik, S.A., & Ayers, T. (2000). Perceived coping efficacy and psychological problems of children of divorce. *Child Development*, 74(4), 1097-1118.

Schaefer, C., & Reid, S. (Eds). (1986). *Game play: Therapeutic use of childhood games*. New York: Wiley.

Solomon, J. (2005). An attachment theory framework for planning infant and toddler visitation arrangements in never-married, separated, and divorced families. In L. Gunsberg & P. Hymowitz (Eds.), *A handbook of divorce and custody: Forensic, developmental, and clinical perspectives*. Analytic Press.

Stolberg, A.L., & Mahler, J. (1994). Enhancing treatment gains in a school-based intervention for children of divorce through skill training, parental involvement, and transfer procedures. *Journal of Consulting Psychology*, 62,147-156.

Sullivan, M. J. and Kelly, J. (2001). Legal and psychological management of cases with an alienated child. *Family and Conciliation Courts Review*, 39 (3), 299-315. (To order contact: www.blackwell-synergy.com)

Sweeney, D. and Homeyer, L. (1999). *Group play therapy*. San Francisco: Jossey-Bass.

Trubitt, A. (2004). Play *therapy goes to court, 2nd Edition: Implications and applications in contested child custody*. Self Published. Available through: www.anitatrubitt.com

Utay, J.M., & Lampe, R.E. (1995). Use of group counseling games to enhance social skills of children with learning disabilities. *Journal for Specialists in Group Work*, 20 (2), 114-120.

Wallerstein, J.S., and Kelly, J.B. (1980). *Surviving the breakup*. New York: Basic Books.

Wallerstein, J.S. (1983). Children of divorce: the psychological tasks of the child. *American Journal of Orthopsychiatry* 53:230-243.

Wallerstein, J.S., and Blakeslee, S. (1989). *Second chances: Men, women, children a decade after divorce*. New York:Ticknor & Fields.

Warshak, R. (2001). Current controversies regarding parental alienation syndrome. *American Journal of Forensic Psychology*, 19, 1-31.

Warshak, R.A. (2002). Misdiagnosis of parental alienation syndrome. *American Journal of Forensic Psychology*, 20, 31-52.

Warshak, R.A. (2003). Bringing sense to parental alienation: A look at the dispute and the evidence. *Family Law Quarterly*, 37, 273-301.

Organizations and Web Sites

American Academy of Child and Adolescent Psychiatry: 202-966-7300; www.aacap.org

American Art Therapy Association: 847-949-6064; www.arttherapy.org

Association For Play Therapy: 559-252-2278; www.a4pt.org

Association of Family and Conciliation Courts: www.afccnet.org

Canadian Art Therapy Association: www.catainfo.ca

Canadian Association For Child And Play Therapy: 800-361-3951; www.cacpt.com

Center for Mental Health Services: 800-789-2647; www.mentalhealth.org

National Child Traumatic Stress Network: www.NCTSNet.org

National Council for Children's Rights: www.gocrc.com

www.KidsHealth.org

www.kidsturn.org

www.uptoparents.org

Suppliers of Therapy Materials

Anna's Toy Depot (toys, doll families, plastic animals): 888-227-9169

Oriental Trading Company (stickers, prizes, novelty items): 800-875-8480

Rose Play Therapy (toys, doll families, plastic animals): 800-713-2252

Stickers: www.esticker.com

ABOUT THE AUTHOR

Liana Lowenstein, MSW, RSW, CPT-S, is a Registered Social Worker and Certified Play Therapy Supervisor in Toronto, Canada. She maintains a private practice, specializing in assessing and treating children with a variety of emotional difficulties, and she conducts Custody and Access Evaluations. In addition to her clinical work, she provides consultation and supervision to mental health practitioners. She lectures internationally on child trauma and play therapy, and she is on the teaching faculty of the Canadian Association for Child & Play Therapy. Ms. Lowenstein is author of numerous publications including the books, *Paper Dolls & Paper Airplanes: Therapeutic Exercises for Sexually Traumatized Children* (Crisci, Lay and Lowenstein, 1997), *Creative Interventions for Troubled Children & Youth* (1999), *More Creative Interventions for Troubled Children & Youth* (2002), and *Creative Interventions for Bereaved Children* (2006).

Also by Liana Lowenstein

Creative Interventions for Troubled Children and Youth

More Creative Interventions for Troubled Children & Youth

Creative Interventions for Bereaved Children

Assessment and Treatment Techniques for Children, Adolescents, and Families: Practitioners Share Their Most Effective Techniques (Volumes One through Three)

Creative Family Therapy Techniques: Play, Art, and Expressive Therapies to Engage Children in Family Sessions

Cory Helps Kids Cope with Divorce: Playful Therapeutic Activities for Young Children"

***For further information about the above books and upcoming publications, go to www.lianalowenstein.com

FREE BONUS GIFT

As a purchaser of **Creative Interventions for Children of Divorce**, you're entitled to a special bonus from Liana Lowenstein.

Now you can get the eBook, **Favorite Therapeutic Activities for Children, Youth, and Families: Practitioners Share Their Most Effective Interventions**. This is a creative collection of assessment and treatment techniques for individual, group, and family therapy.

To download the eBook, go here now:

www.lianalowenstein.com

On the home page, you will see where to click to get the free eBook

You can also sign up to receive my **free monthly online newsletter**. Every newsletter contains fresh and relevant content including new articles, featured counseling techniques, discounts on mental health resources, and more.

Sign-up for the newsletter at: www. lianalowenstein.com

Enjoy your free resources!

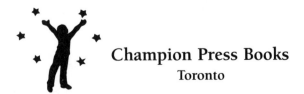

Champion Press Books
Toronto